Bad Dreams

Notes on Life and Los Angeles
by a Would-Be Has-Been

Jenny Noa

Design and interior layout by Ryan Mulford.

ISBN 979-8-9917609-0-4 (paperback)

ISBN 979-8-9917609-1-1 (ebook)

www.jennynoa.com

Author's Note

The pieces that formed the initial framework for this book were written for live storytelling or essay show performances when I lived in LA, so those may be familiar to anyone attending shows in that era. I've added new material in addition to some other pieces that were until now known only to close friends and a small handful of readers of my blog.

In this book, I discuss mental illness, mild OCD related to a body image disorder, weight issues, depression, anxiety, grief, and the deaths of a spouse, a parent, and a pet. There is some cursing.

We are not always compassionate with ourselves and my effort to be truthful about my own experiences may cause unintentional pain to others dealing with similar issues. I sincerely hope that is not the case, but please proceed carefully.

*For those with unrealized creative dreams
and/or undiagnosed mental disorders.*

Stages

Intentionally Left Blank

Carcinojenny

Body of Work

Corpses of Hollywood

Consolation

Stage One:

Intentionally Left Blank

Scooch Down

WHEN I WAS FOUR years old, I woke up in the middle of the night and threw up on my own pillow. This was practically unheard of. Mine was an iron constitution. I can recall every vomit of my childhood, it was that rare.

I was a rule follower and non-complainer, a blue-ribbon member of the clean plate club. You could count on me. But I'd thrown up on my own pillow. If ever there were a reason to wake up the household at four years old, this was a pretty good one.

"Dad," I said in a near whisper. "Dad."

You probably noticed that I called for my dad and not my mom. At the tender age of barely coherent, I already knew that he was the one who would show up no matter who we called.

Obviously, he didn't hear me. I shared a room with one of my two sisters, and she didn't even wake up. I couldn't reasonably put my foot on the floor in the middle of the night (monsters) or walk through the dark hallway (ghosts), so I did the only thing left to do. I scooched down in the bed and went back to sleep.

I threw up on my own pillow and *went back to sleep*.

That's all anyone needs to know about me. In the wrong hands, it's a dangerous piece of information, but I've noticed most people can just tell by looking. Is it pathological self-sufficiency, or something much, much more pathetic? Why not both?

I think I was born timid and accommodating, and I'd had enough early lessons in my mother's volatility and anger to cement those traits. By this point, nature and nurture were probably neck-and-neck. And the early 70s were a vastly different time in terms of child rearing. I like to think that if I were a parent and had a clear warning sign like this one, I'd work hard to try to course correct my little weirdo. I never had kids of my own, but it seems like simple math: if a child can't call for help when she's in trouble — you can bet the adult won't be able to either.

I don't know how I could have done it differently. How that little kid could have done it differently. I got good at it, at scooching down and going back to sleep. Not just reluctant to ask, but afraid to. Because not getting something you want is par for the course. Asking and still not getting it, at least for me, hurts like knives. I learned not to speak up because I didn't want to be that little girl whispering in the dark to no one. But I forgot she wasn't asking for all that much.

At fifteen years old, I woke up late on the night of a knee operation to realize that I hadn't peed for roughly fourteen hours, since before the surgery that morning. Then I learned that the nurses' call button wasn't attached to anything. So here I was again. "Nurse," I stage-whispered. But I could not bring myself to inconvenience my three sleeping roommates by shouting. None of them would've hesitated to wake me if the situation were reversed, and I'd have held no grudge if they had. They were baffled by the story the next morning. So was I. Nevertheless.

I am constitutionally incapable of making a fuss on my own behalf. This complicates things quite a lot. As a caregiver for my husband during his cancer, I was called upon to be his champion. I loved Mark, and I know I did everything I could do to extend his life and make him comfortable. But I drew a line at pitching a screaming tantrum in the ER waiting room, which, thanks to Shirley MacLaine's performance in *Terms of Endearment*, is the weird gold standard for devotion and care.

It's one thing not to think I count, but surely *he* did? The problem is that, for me, so did everyone else in that emergency room. And to say *Take him* was to also say *That person should wait even longer,* and *This person doesn't matter as much.*

Oh, to be seen. To get the prize because I deserve it, or failing that, because I'm *next*. Why can't life be fair? Why did I have to beg the ER triage nurse to take my husband next? He was vomiting into the pink bucket they'd given us an hour before. For the record, I *did* beg, and seeing as how she still thought the others should go first, then I'm guessing that they were pretty sick, no? Because there is always a worse hard luck story than yours in the ER, always. It's not a game you want to win.

On one of many of our trips to the ER over almost four years, a man came running in demanding immediate help for his friend, who was having a stroke. He apparently knew the signs to watch for from that email we all got about stroke symptoms, you know the one. Even his friend was telling him to cool it, but the guy kept on yelling at the woman behind the glass until finally they took him back. And the guy who brought him in walked up and down the room, talking loudly to no one and everyone about how shocking it is that they would dare to make him wait, when clearly it was an emergency. And we all just stared at him, a frozen and miserable tableau, and poor Mark sat there with his bucket. What did that guy think the rest of us were doing there? But I have to give him credit: he did the thing I couldn't do — forget that there was anyone else in the world as important as his friend. And he won.

Mark felt terrible afterward, but there was a moment that day when he turned to me and said, "Help me." I was doing everything I could, and it still wasn't enough. I can't make people do what I want them to do. I couldn't make him go to the doctor when the first symptoms appeared; if I'd been successful, neither of us would have been in the ER at all.

It has been pointed out to me that in situations like these, we are all reduced to a child-like dependency on the authority figure in charge. Our reactions are informed by our relationships with our parents, and all roads for me lead to my mother, who didn't pick us first, who never came in the middle of the night when we needed her. But why can't people just know you need them? Why should we have to spell it out?

Other people rarely come through, whether they are biologically invested in your survival or even contractually obligated to take care of you. What if my dad *did* hear me call? It was the middle of the night. He could easily have thought that holding out for a minute might mean the problem would fix itself. And it did.

I say I don't ask, but I do. I've learned to ask for what I want at an audible volume, for starters. I don't yell it at customer service reps, or the odd healthcare professional, but I can make my wishes known. The problem is that it usually doesn't get me anywhere.

There's no guarantee, after all. In fact, I've got a terrible return rate on my asks, which frankly feels personal. How could it feel anything but?

In response, I ask less and less often. Which in turn makes the rejections even more painful. This is usually about jobs — day jobs and auditions. But it's not the loss of the job that hurts. It's that I asked. Even though I understand that there are vast pools of applicants and a shit ton of politics. It's not personal. But I *asked*. *She* asked. There's an extra layer of mortification because I've made myself vulnerable.

Sometimes I self-scooch and sometimes scooching is thrust upon me.

Some people have a healthy fuck-you response to a lack of care — they can demand better, or ask often enough to average out some meaningful successes. Me, I scooch. But making do with next to nothing is only admirable in very narrow circumstances. On the space station, I'd be employee of the year. Regular society doesn't even notice it. They get real used to it, though. My speaking up is met with indifference, irritation, or a total lack of acknowledgement that I've spoken at all. I'm expected to just do what I've always done. Be quiet. Do what I was doing, or come up with makeshift solutions with the tools at hand, but for goodness sake, do it quietly and without complaint.

When Mark was sick, I had all kinds of well-intentioned, lovely, generous people, poised to do anything I needed, and they were mostly frustrated and baffled by my seeming refusal to take them up on it. But what I really needed — a cure for cancer, a time machine, financial stability — no one could give me. I had the smaller stuff under control. Partly, I was just good at doing without. I was also a human Jenga tower. I couldn't let anyone do anything to help without feeling like it would all come apart. Once you start to lean, you'll fall.

If you do manage to call loud enough, is the right person going to hear? Will anyone come? And if you dig deep and ask the one you really want for something you think you need, what are the odds that they'll have that thing *and* be willing to give it to you? Or that you'll be able to do the same for them? It seems sort of impossible. And it all presses on this giant open wound of mine, which may be too late to heal.

I learned very young not to need very much, certainly not anything I couldn't get for myself. But I don't recommend it. You *can* live on bread alone, but it's just bread. Getting by is the only prize you get when you can't advocate for yourself. When all the major decisions of your life are made by other people.

Honestly, my certainty that I don't deserve as much as the next guy makes me eminently suitable for low-level office work and long-term patient caregiving. In both cases, extremely low expectations will probably serve me in the end. Shirley MacLaine's character was completely irrational, she lost her shit in that movie. You think she could have held on for four years? I don't have a breaking point when it comes to sucking it up, so I guess that's the bright side.

Bit Part: Make 'em Laugh

IN ONE OF MY earliest memories, my mother holds me as we arrive at a neighbor's house. I'm three years old, sucking not my thumb, but my index finger — palm up, the pad of the finger up against the palate. Try it, it's a great fit.

"Hi, Florence," the neighbor says.

"Hello," says my mom.

Out pops my finger. I know what comes next. "Would you like some coffee?" I say.

They laugh. They *laugh*.

Maybe I already know that my mother is angry almost all the time. Maybe I'm basking in adult attention, or I recognize that laughter is magic. Maybe it's all the above.

The Answer

New experiences have always caused me a lot of anxiety. Doing a brand new thing in a place I've never been or where I will need to find parking inspires a lot of internal angst. It's a convergence of multiple issues — outsized safety concerns, an OCD body image disorder, and garden-variety anxiety. This isn't as much of a concern when I'm with someone else, however; I do better with human buffers, sharing the stage as it were. I'm just not a solo adventurer. There are ways to deal with this — lots of preparation, way-finding research, street-level views, and early departures. I break everything down into small, discrete steps, and I give myself permission to opt out at any time. But I'm still a nervous wreck, which I compensate for in different ways.

I was a terrible little ass-kisser in elementary school, for example.

In the early 1970s, I started at a new school for second grade, and Mrs. N was my teacher. I was truly frightened of her. Mrs. N was in her sixties and a stubborn holdover from the corporal punishment days. My older sister told me how Mrs. N had hit her on top of her head because of how many questions she'd gotten wrong on a quiz. This was especially scary, not only because Lisa kindly demonstrated on my head just how hard she was hit, but because it *hadn't been Lisa's quiz.* Mrs. N had asked the students to trade quizzes with the person across from them in order to check their work. She saw the score and lashed out. Then she apologized to Lisa and ran around to the other desk to hit the right kid.

Heading to this new school, all I knew for sure was that I could and probably would be physically hit by a grown-up if I strayed out of line – *or even if I didn't.* I had no choice but to begin ingratiating myself with Mrs. N from day one, a defense mechanism only the most pathetic and fearful are capable of. I had some experience with mercurial and somewhat frightening grownups, after all. I hugged her each day upon arrival. I volunteered for every task. I finished my work as soon as possible. I was careful to stay inside the lines.

Because I was a colossal suck-butt, one day I was rewarded when she said that since I'd completed my work, I could check my answers against the Teacher's Edition. I felt like I had arrived.

I decided to crime. I realized that I could just write down tomorrow's answers from the Teacher's Edition and save myself some work and no small amount of anxiety. So I did. The pressure was getting to me; I was chafing at the Perfect Child bonds that I had tied myself up in. I rationalized that because my answers were almost always right anyway, this crime was victimless. I felt I should get extra credit for thinking of this.

I can't reconcile this except to say that being an anxious seven-year-old is utterly exhausting. I needed some relief.

It wasn't my first offense. There was a period when I'd regularly ingested my parents' prescription medication from the bathroom cabinet. Even then, I was the soul of moderation. Small enough to perch on the bathroom sink, I would carefully choose that night's pharmaceutical. But I took just one pill from each bottle, and I spaced them out. (More on this in the section titled "How to Muffle Your Own Cry for Attention.") This lasted till I asked my mother what bloating was and had no answer for where I'd heard the word. Nothing is out of the reach of children.

But this new crime was heady. When the time came to offer our answers to the next day's assignment, I was, for the first time in my young life, confident in my answers. I knew what I said would be correct, because my answers came from the Teacher's Edition. There was no higher authority.

My hand shot up, and of course Mrs. N called on me, her little darling. "Jenny, what did you write for question number one?"

I cleared my throat. "Answers may vary," I said.

"I beg your pardon?"

"Answers ..." I trailed off, *finally* stopping to consider what I had said.

She did not hit me on the head. She was across the room, so it was inconvenient, but she didn't need to. I could feel myself deflating, turning back into a small, meek lump, scarred for life.

It certainly saved me from any more criminal activity, so soundly was I punished for my transgression. It is a humiliation I still feel, half a century later. It hurt to write this.

But I try to take my lessons from hardship, and you can't do much better than this one. On elementary school worksheets and beyond, answers may vary.

Fault Lines

I'M TOLD THAT PEOPLE speak their minds either because they want to get something off their chest, or because they want to effect some change. I don't see the point of unburdening for its own sake. I need it to mean something to the listener, but to expect change just because you've spoken is naïve. I can't believe these are our only choices.

We all end up in conversations with people who aren't listening or just don't care. You're lucky to get a pat on the head. "Thank you," they say. "Noted. Point taken." And then they do whatever they were going to do anyway. Which is the same as not having listened at all.

Most of us have people in our lives who truly care about what we have to say, who try to understand us, and may even modify some behavior as a result. But it's rare. My god, it's rare.

When I was 16 years old, my family went through some lean times. My dad had started his own graphic design business a few years before, and though he'd had a very successful first year or so, things were now more down than up. Christmas was especially down. Money issues made my mother more snappish than usual, because as an artist she made demands on the finances with only intermittent returns. I don't hold that against her; she was a brilliant artist, and I believe the investment was well worth it. But her own unacknowledged guilt made her moody and on edge, and she directed those feelings at my sisters and me, especially if she thought we were being frivolous with money.

She also disliked Christmas, for lots of reasons, and that cast a pall over the season no matter how festive we tried to be. We threw whole parties that she spent alone upstairs in her room, "not feeling well." It was practically gothic, the angry woman upstairs, haunting the house, at odds with everyone else. It wasn't her holiday to begin with, as she was raised Jewish, and she also had very strong feelings about consumerism and ungrateful children. I think she also resented happy families, and we celebrated with my dad's warm and loving clan. I can see that it was a lot for her to bear.

On a cold winter's day during the peak of holiday shopping season, my younger sister Elena, then thirteen, went to the mall with a friend. She took with her fifty dollars my dad had given her to buy gifts. My father and I drove to pick them up and we were almost home when the awful discovery was made. Elena had left her purse at the mall. The purse with the fifty dollars still inside it. Though we knew it was probably pointless, it was decided that the three of them would drive back on the slim chance that the purse might still be there, and that I would go in and tell my mother what had happened.

I approached her lair, the den where she was watching TV. I said, "Um. Just so you know, Elena left her purse behind at the mall. They went back to see if it's still there."

"Oh, my GOD," Mom said. "Was the fifty dollars in there?"

"Uh, yes?"

"Jesus CHRIST."

"Well," I said, "It wasn't her fault ...."

She cut me off. "How can you say it wasn't her fault?"

I tried to undo the terrible thing I'd done. "Well, yes, it's her *fault*, but she didn't mean to do it, is all I meant."

"Tell me how this isn't her fault."

"I'm not saying it isn't, I'm just—"

"You just said it's not her fault."

"But I added more stuff ...."

Alas, it was in vain. My mother continued to wonder aloud whose fault I could imagine it was, if not Elena's, the criminal in question. I tried again to say, "No, no, it's her fault," just to end the conversation, even though it wasn't true. Leaving the purse behind may have been careless, or irresponsible. But it was also accidental. She was thirteen.

Things escalated. For roughly forty-five minutes, we had several verbal bouts, separated by my furious stomping up the stairs to my room, where I shored up my reserves and stomped back down for another go. Anthropologically speaking, this has parallels with today's online comment threads. It was as pointless and enraging in its live-action form.

When my father finally returned, I was screaming, "IT'S HER FAULT, IT'S HER FAULT!" over and over, at capacity volume.

I paused for breath, and my mother turned to my dad and said, "Can you believe it? Jenny doesn't think it's her fault."

I don't know how I lived to tell this tale, or more to the point, how she did, but something broke in me. Miraculously, not the veins in my neck, or my larynx, but something big. I am still learning how big.

Because everyone needs to be heard, to feel like what they are saying matters. And I think it can drive one to extremes. My mother didn't get it as a child, and it made her incapable of hearing others. I felt the need so deeply, I was convinced I should pursue a career in acting. I wanted an audience.

Not feeling heard by my own mother was deeply painful and frustrating. She had a colossal amount of shit to shovel, and I feel for her, but that is not my fault. It felt pointless to talk to her, to maintain any sort of relationship. I left the house a year later for college, and I stayed as far away as I could for as long as possible, but I never got anywhere. My relationship with my mother certainly didn't improve, and my plan to be heard from stages and screens failed.

It shows up everywhere. For example, I don't submit these written pieces for traditional publication. It's easy to think it's the typical rejection from an editor that I'm afraid of — *we read it but didn't like it* — but I'm more concerned that they don't read it at all. How can I be sure you're giving it your full attention; how can you understand what I'm saying if you can't hear my voice? A query letter? What, am I supposed to *beg?* I'm not going to *ask.* What would be the point of that? No really, I want to know.

Auditions are another example. What a word, audition. The act of hearing. The irony of trying in vain to get people to see and hear you, even though they are talking or texting, or eating lunch, and have probably already cast the part. It's dehumanizing, and I don't have it in me.

To say that it's gotten in my way is an understatement. A coworker once expressed an interest in coming to see me read at a show, and I did what I usually do. I gently and persistently gave her a list of reasons she might not want to: You don't have to. No pressure! This maybe won't be the best show for you to see. It's ten dollars! It's so hard to find parking. I'll keep you posted.

Finally, she said, "Stop telling me not to come to your show."

No one should feel obligated to see me perform, and if by chance someone decides to come anyway, I will test their will to do so.

I once wrote and produced a solo show and I could barely bring myself to tell anyone about it. It took *years* for that show to get to stage. Each essay is a difficult birth. I feel a sense of triumph when something finally gets said, but the danger is that I feel like I'm owed something for having spoken. People are not required to listen harder, or care, just because something has been torn from me with difficulty. That struggle is my problem, and it comes with no guarantees. It's the biggest hurdle I face.

My favorite Dr. Suess book was *Horton Hears a Who*. Why? Because Horton HEARS A WHO. Because a person's a person no matter how small! In that book, that littlest, most reluctant Who finally speaks in the end, and they are all heard because he does. And what are they yelling? "We are here! We are here! We are here!" The same thing we're all yelling. But that Who's little voice is the tipping point. His voice matters.

I loved that story as a child, but I fear I took the wrong message to heart. It matters that you speak, of course, but not to everyone. Seldom will it save the world. The world is mostly yelling its own things.

I write mini rants and post them to what is essentially a secret blog that I don't tell anyone about. Speaking where virtually no one can hear, into a void. Maybe it's therapeutic. Maybe I'm building up that muscle. If there's no expectation on my end, there's no crushing disappointment. And it's so nice to be stumbled upon. Found. Heard by a total stranger. Where the words mean something and I as a person am out of the mix entirely. It's a pure exchange.

It's fair to say it's my mother's fault that I write things the hell down. When the only other person in the room cannot hear you at any decibel, well, you must find another way. It's also why, when asked for directions, or to describe a sequence of events, I will give the most detailed, blow-by-blow account you have ever heard. If you're really listening, well then, I'll reward you with all the details you can stand.

I've spent a lot of time trying to figure out why I couldn't seem to pursue acting, find an agent, or publish my writing. But there are other rewards. I wrote all this down, for example. I read these pieces around town in various settings, and there is nothing that really compares (not surprisingly) to reading something I wrote to people who have elected to hear it. I don't even know how they heard of the show or why they are there, and I don't want to. They came, they're listening, and all I can do is hold up my end of the bargain the best way I know how. It's a sacred contract for me.

So, thank you, thank you for listening. It means the world.

Safer to Walk

I SIMPLY DO NOT understand adventurers and explorers. Even the excessively curious are a matter of curiosity to me. But those are the people virtually every story is written about. I know because I read quite a bit.

Adventurers are people who say *yes*. I am a *no* person. It's my first, knee-jerk answer. I love the indoors.

There are no praises to sing about us *no* people. We might go along on your adventure, but only because we were caught up in the tide, or because a *yes* person felt like they had to be polite, or more likely they needed someone to call ahead about lodging and fold the maps. We *no* people will hold the jackets and backpacks while the others have fun. Waiting on benches at fun parks is a particular skill of mine.

It's been handed down through the generations. Each side has a long and illustrious *no* history. My paternal grandmother's hair was snow white by the time she was thirty-five. When I asked why, the answer was "worry." On the other side, my mother's father was a miserable, stern, unyielding asshole. He embodied the word *no*.

It's a dynasty. My folks were the Duke and Duchess of Why Don't We Just Stay In. It had a formative impact on me and my sisters, naturally. Two cerebral, unadventurous adults with big *no* energy will breed three homebodies inordinately interested in the domestic arts.

My mother was a gifted artist, and really driven to do her work to the exclusion of everything else, including us. Though she was technically an at-home mom, she wasn't really available to us. When I think about her during these years, the image that comes to mind is the closed basement door. It wasn't locked. We could visit her studio, but we couldn't need her for anything. A ride anywhere was off the table, so our summertime fun area was bound by the parks we could walk to. You can see how easily the circle shrinks.

A tactic she employed rather often was to convince the asker that the thing they wanted was dangerous or bad. Her stance on driving when it was raining or snowing was that it was actually safer to walk. The irony is that this was almost always true — she was a terrible driver.

Printed in my sixth-grade yearbook was a list of graduating students' aspirations. My near-term goal involved working in a vet's office when I was old enough, which my mother had okayed, "as long as it is within walking distance." This line is printed in the yearbook. That's how much it was burned into our brains.

No, let's not. We'll see. Hm, no.

When I was old enough to babysit, I also only had one answer. "Can we stay up past our bedtime?" No. "Can we play outside?" No. "Can we—" No. I think I thought I was following the rules, but I was really just terrified at the enormous responsibility of keeping these people alive. And I was bred to say no.

I said no to every opportunity that came along. It took a while for me to figure things out, to test my limits, realize what I was capable of. I mean, I think boundaries are good, it's just that they were all I had.

But it was the 70s, so that is not entirely true. We had tremendous freedom in ways that would now border on negligence, but that was how most children were raised back then. Among our friend group, your parents had to have a general idea of where to look for you if they ever needed you (they didn't), and otherwise you just had to be home by dinnertime. You could show up filthy and bleeding, but woe betide anyone who was late for dinner.

There was a park quite close to our house, but to get there, you had to cross what my mother deemed a Busy Street, which we weren't allowed to cross by ourselves. We were encouraged to get out of the house, but we were also required to call for one of the summertime park counselors to come and help us cross. The three of us would stand there, screaming for Corky and Candy (real names), until one of them saw fit to stub out their cigarette on the scarred picnic table and come save us. I always figured they couldn't hear us, but I've been back there as an adult, and they definitely, definitely could.

They probably thought we'd give up eventually and cross by ourselves, but they obviously didn't know who they were dealing with. Still, who would leave little kids to stand there screaming? But also, who wouldn't walk their kids down the block to the park? And what kids wouldn't summon the defiance needed to look both ways?

Times have changed a lot since then, and my sisters and I were always together and lucky that nothing ever happened to us. We were three little girls, almost always walking by ourselves. This could easily be an abduction story, a Lifetime movie with a colon in the title. I Grew Up With Strangers: The Jenny Noa Story.

Phelp's Park, the closest one with a pool, could be reached by following along that same Busy Road we weren't allowed to cross. I wonder now if it was a whole mile away, or did it just seem that long? I was seven, and wearing those wooden Dr. Scholl's sandals, so it might as well have been a hundred.

One time, Lisa went to the park down the hill with our neighbor, her playmate, and they stopped at a friend's house on the way back. They stayed there for a bit, playing in the front yard, but she got snitched on by a passing neighbor. She got in trouble, essentially for not being either at the park or traveling to or from it. Never mind that it was the only part of their journey where they'd been in proximity to a responsible adult.

These little infractions were punished at a level that deterred future defiance — for me. Lisa had no problem withstanding the usual lectures and being sent to her room. She had defiance to spare. But the yelling, my god, the yelling. I didn't want any part of any of that.

On the few occasions my parents would go out, they'd say, "Now, you girls go to bed by eight, do you hear?" And we *would*. Bound to the *no* people, with fear as the glue. It was mostly, as I said, convenience. They didn't have to worry if they knew we were right there. Mom didn't have to pay much attention or give up any time. And I know she never thought it would do real damage. Oh, but they did congratulate themselves and accept praise. All anyone could say was what great girls we were. We were the best little shut-ins. So well-behaved.

Years later, my mother would shake her head at me. "Jenny, what are you so afraid of?"

Everything, Mom. Every damn thing.

I am clinically anxious, but it's a nature/nurture thing. All the usual go-tos for a frightened primitive brain — *You are alone. Nothing is entirely safe. You are going to get yelled at. No one is coming to get you.* — were, in my case, absolutely 100% true.

One day the skies just opened up at the pool, a torrential downpour. We trudged toward home with our hairbrushes rolled up in soggy towels. All the other parents picked up their kids, and one mom stopped and asked, visibly alarmed, if she could please drive us home. But we knew we could no more accept a ride from a stranger than cross a Busy Street alone. Lisa, soaking wet, over the sound of the rain, yelled, "Thanks! But it's safer to walk!"

Corners

NATURALLY, WE HAD GAMES that could be played in the house. I remember one we made up called Fred. It consisted of one of us crawling headfirst into a pillowcase, wedging into the space behind the pillow. The other two would twirl the pillowed one around a few times and then laugh while the dizzy one bumped into stuff. Good old Fred.

The Bronte sisters we were not, but Fred was hilarious.

My favorite game, hands down, was Corners. This was a rainy-day kind of game, where we'd clear the crap out of a corner of our room and string up a sheet or a towel, or pull the bed away from the wall, and make a little tented space. It was my own separate peace, away from the fighting and volatility that could be happening in another part of the house. I was content to sit in my corner and read or think, whatever. Elena always wanted me to visit her corner, or have her over to mine, but I never wanted more than to just be. I still have a little note she sent via the Corners town mail service. In it she asks nicely if I'd like to come by, but I checked the "no" box and, presumably, sent it back via the post.

I wasn't hiding from getting yelled at by my mother — my anxiety was about *when*. It was about the total unpredictability of her moods. It was about not knowing what lay ahead, what dinner would bring, how my immediate future would be shaped.

Which perhaps explains a little about my reticence to do new things on my own, my anxieties about new places, and why I like nothing more than a step-by-step guide. I was absolutely dreading a recent colonoscopy until they gave me the sheaf of instructions. I pored over them like I would a pirate map. You do this, then this, then that? Okay, then, poop chute, let's do this! And then I told everyone who'd listen all about the process (edited, I promise) because I assumed that demystifying the unknown is as important to them as it is to me.

Of course, doing nothing at all — and being free of the kind of danger my mother represented for me — was what winning felt like. Peace and quiet, no demands, no raised voices. That was the prize I was after. And that followed me into adulthood. If I can get home as quickly as possible, sit in the same spot on the couch, and enjoy reading quietly in near-total isolation, it can feel like I achieved something.

This does not dovetail neatly with a life on the stage or auditioning or any of the other things I said I wanted. Looking back, I've done almost nothing without wishing it was over already so I could be home where it's quiet. If my stated goal was for a vibrant and creative life on stage or screen, my efforts went to peace and safety. I was frustrated because I felt like I was sabotaging myself, but my subconscious knew what I needed. I just couldn't make sense of it.

And no wonder I can't seem to step out from the crowd, can't promote myself or my work in any way. Raising my head over the firing line just isn't in me. I've dreamt, like most people have, about a windfall — lottery wins, selling a screenplay — and the end game in these daydreams is always the same: a little cottage somewhere where I can be by myself, read romances, and garden a bit. I'll call it Corners.

Creama Wheat

On Saturdays, when we were kids, my dad brought us into New York City, a short jaunt from our suburban New Jersey town, to stay overnight with our grandparents. These were my father's parents, the Puerto Rican side of the family. In temperament and big-heartedness, they were the opposite of my mother's folks. They were unfailingly kind to Mom, which only seemed to grate on her, and so her relationship with her in-laws frayed over time just as almost every one of her relationships did.

My dad's parents were loving and indulgent with my sisters and me, as many grandparents are, and they were deeply in love with each other. Their home was among the safest spaces of my childhood. Their love for us was unconditional, and they even seemed to like having us around, never mind that my grandmother waited on us hand and foot. It was like finding out you're really a princess, but every weekend.

At home, we had absurdly early bedtimes. In the summer, the sun was often still up when we went to bed, and we could hear our friends playing outside. It was impossible not to feel like our parents had simply had enough of us. At Grandma's, though, we were welcome to stay up late, and we all squeezed on the couch to watch the Saturday night line-up, including *The Mary Tyler*

Moore Show, *The Bob Newhart Show*, and *The Carol Burnett Show*. The importance of these cannot be overstated.

Crucially, we were with Grandma for sometimes as many as four or five meals. It wasn't just that she could cook, and she really could, it's that she *would*. There was nothing she couldn't cook well, but when I asked my sisters recently what they remembered best, it was the simplest foods. Lisa said her brownies, Elena her white rice. For me, it was Cream of Wheat, or Creama, as we called it for short. Creama Wheat. I remember standing in the kitchen doorway and looking up at her as she made it. It took forever. There were no shortcuts, no instant mixes. She stirred that pot with such focus, so much attention, it was like she tended a living thing. In fact, that's exactly what she was doing.

The kindest thing I can hope for you is that someone, someday, cooks for you the way my grandmother cooked for us, as if there were no more important thing in the world. Her meals told us *we* were important; each was a gift of love. I think she saved our lives in a way. I'm not sure how we'd have ended up if we hadn't known what that kind of devotion felt like. So, although this sounds like it's about food, it isn't. It's about nourishment. And lucky for us, just a little bit was enough to grow up strong.

Very Amusing

We three Noa girls share a sense of humor. The true balm of being together is the laughing we do. Laughter is medicine, but you need the good stuff. The bent-over-at-the-waist, flared-nostril, wheezy-noise laughter so few get enough of. That's what we have.

My dad was the funny parent. He could be goofy for our sakes, and looking back, that was such a gift. He was the easy-going, slow-to-anger one, and far less likely to make a mountain out of a molehill. We fought to hold his hand when we were little, and when we were older, we appealed to him as the reasonable one to intercede in fights with our mom. But we also just liked to hang out with him, because he was so reliably even keeled. He was an anchor.

Maybe we learned our sense of humor from him, because we laughed at the same things he did: weird turns of phrase, odd little things no one else seemed to notice. It was a language we all spoke, which of course is bound to leave people out.

My mother was probably dismayed by his gravitational pull. She was also just plain angry about a lot of things. Our household looked like a lot of others in the 1970s. He worked while she was home, and I think she resented the way he sailed in at the end of the day and basked in the adoration of the daughters with whom she'd been at odds since he'd left that morning.

It wasn't in her to try to find common ground, to try to understand opposing perspectives, or process her resentment in a healthy way. If she didn't choose the TV program, she'd sit stonily, wondering aloud what she was missing in the way of *Masterpiece Theater* or intellectually edifying documentaries. And inevitably, after something cracked the rest of us up, after we'd laughed and wiped our eyes and sighed happily, she'd deadpan after exactly one beat — really, her timing in this was impeccable — "Very amusing," in a tone that conveyed just how unamusing she found it. It was something she seemed proud of, to be the lone person who found nothing funny about anything at all.

That's probably not fair, because she did laugh sometimes. My dad could cajole her and tease her out of her moods. But there was something about all of us together that changed things. I can't remember any time when we all laughed together … I'm sure it happened. I'm sure it did.

"Very amusing" was her best joke. We thought it was hilarious.

It's painful to think about how alone she must have felt. But she made it so difficult to include her in anything. She was the definition of hard to please, and she seemed wired for anger. I don't think she was capable of anything else, and it's heartbreaking. She came by it honestly — her father's immigration to the U.S. as a child was prompted by violent tragedy, and there was nothing done to process that horror and grief. Humorlessness is probably the least of what gets passed on through the generations.

But I learned from her. One of her constant exhortations was "People should love you for who you are," but she was so angry and mercurial — everything she was said "keep out." And though she certainly expected people to love her as she was, no matter what, her regard for you clearly faltered when you displeased her or disagreed.

I set out to make every single person love me, to get on their good side from the start by being helpful and accommodating and funny. But she just thought it was her due. And we did love her, of course we did. But she made it so much harder than it had to be. It's wearying to love people who rarely seem to love you back, or who have so many conditions attached.

And in a cruel twist of fate, it was only in her illness that she became more fun to be around, more easy going, quicker to laugh. It was a glimpse, perhaps, of the person that had been inside of her all that time. One who was finally able to get past all the anger and hurt, who maybe looked around at us laughing together and liked what she saw.

Bit Part: Union Strong

My mother made her life as simple as possible. She was primarily interested in making art, and far less in knowing exactly where we were or preparing our meals. Mom was particularly resentful that she had to stop work to make dinner. She was a competent cook, just uninspired and apt to take shortcuts afforded by things like the microwave and pressure cooker. Our oven died one day when I was in my early teens, and it wasn't replaced for three full years.

Look, I get it. I'm annoyed about the effort it takes just to keep myself fed. Watching my friends go through the never-ending cycle of planning, prepping, cooking, and cleaning, sometimes multiple times a day to largely indifferent audiences, I can see it's a grind a lot of the time. But it's also the minimum. Kids need to eat.

We were not sufficiently grateful, it seems, and so she turned the dinner preparation burden over to us, not by teaching us how to cook, or by instituting a shared chore system, but by bowing out entirely. "I'm on strike," she'd announce upon emerging from her basement art studio, and then she'd lie down on the couch.

This meant we were charged with making dinner for the family. She may have been on strike, but one of her demands was a hearty, timely dinner, complete with protein, starch, and a vegetable. She had standards. During one last-minute walk-out of hers, we scrambled to throw together dinner — Dad brought home Kentucky Fried Chicken, and I made potatoes and some cauliflower.

Mom looked with distaste at the plate I handed her. "It's all beige."

Well, young lady, when you cook dinner, you can make whatever you like.

High School Boys

A GOOD FRIEND OF mine was a year ahead at school and, whether by agreement or coincidence, her male friends saw me as a project. I'm sure I stood out, because I was Not Like Other Girls; I did not dress like them or seek the same social status. My introduction to these older boys was probably my first botched audition. "She talks too much about herself," was the consensus. It would not be the last time I heard that criticism.

It's true that I was all too happy to talk about what was going on in my head. That was partly because of the mysteries of my brain chemistry but also to throw focus from my body. *This one's got some dents and scratches, sure, but let's take a look under the hood.* I was an overeager salesperson.

Taking my larger size with my stated lack of confidence and my obvious poor wardrobe options, well, how could they help themselves? "Jenny, when you moved that way, I could almost tell you were a girl," one of them said, etching it into my brain. I don't blame them entirely, I submitted to it. I wanted to be in their club. I felt lucky that the club members were willing to mentor me.

I had a body image disorder that wouldn't be diagnosed for another three decades. I felt bombarded by images on television, insidious advertising, and personal directives from everyone from my own mother to these friends of a friend. My brain just couldn't make sense of it all, and I felt completely divorced from my body. That these teenage boys were the wrong fixers was obvious to me even then, but what choice did I have? They were part of the larger group that I wanted to please and belong to. The prevailing opinion was that I wasn't quite good enough but, with a little work, not entirely hopeless.

I was not especially girly, for a few reasons. One was simple economics; I couldn't afford to look the part. But even if that weren't a factor, I couldn't bear to be exposed. To walk around in something I felt beautiful in was like walking around naked, it bared my desires in a way that made me miserable. I couldn't allow it then, and I still can't. To wear a daring outfit, or even a trendy new blouse, seemed to be asking people to look at me, and it suggested that I liked how I looked and that others should like it, too. The gremlin inside me screamed, among other even worse things, "HOW DARE YOU. YOU'RE WRONG. NO ONE CAN LOOK AT YOU AND LIKE WHAT THEY SEE."

I had a crush on a boy who didn't know who I was — I mean that, we had no common friends or classes — and my friend let it leak to a friend of his that I liked him. I'm sure she thought she was helping, but I wanted to die, just shrivel up and die. I still don't know how I ever went back to school after that. I rerouted all the pathways and staircases I took between classes, and I stopped visiting friends who shared his homeroom. I'd been using them, I realized, to put myself in his field of vision. My new plan was simply to hope that my total lack of interest would make him think that it was a mistake, an unfounded rumor. I never looked at him again or sought him out in the crowd.

It got a little better for me with my husband, whose open regard for both my insides and outsides helped to balance some of what my inner voices said. He's gone now, and I'm back where I started. I'm sure people wonder at my persistent solitude. But I still can't think of a worse thing than to lay my heart, attached to this body, at someone's feet.

Intentionally Left Blank

My MOTHER WAS A very opinionated person. Which is to say, she thought she was right about everything. She was ready at any time to deliver a lecture or searing indictment of anything in a broad range of subjects — politics, religion, your personal choices — and all she required was your total agreement.

For years I couldn't utter an opinion about anything, to anyone. In most cases, I couldn't even form one. I've written elsewhere about how impossible opposing her was, how exhausting and futile. It took a toll.

There are things we can all complain about when it comes to our childhoods, and no parent is perfect; shitty things happen. My mother had always said that she'd have been a battered child if only her father had been home more, and she had just enough self-awareness to refrain from physical violence, outside of the occasional swat. But, god, she could yell. She could make herself so much bigger that way, the biggest. And I don't think she realized the effect that can have, when you're so very small and the much larger people you depend on for security and love are also screaming at you. What are your options, as a tiny person? Everyone reacts in their own way, of course, and I learned how to observe, defuse, keep quiet, and make people laugh. These things have all served me, but they are also coping mechanisms, and I won't ever know what those things edged out. What has surviving cost me, and in what other directions might I have grown?

Other people called me sensitive all the time, even when I was really little, and it's a label that has followed me around. But "sensitive" is often what you call someone when you don't want to apologize. Am I sensitive, or was I responding to circumstances?

Both. The answer is both.

Growing up in my mother's house, it seemed wise to suspend judgment, to wait, gauge the reactions of the others, and fit myself in somewhere acceptable to all parties. And, man, I was good at it. In this way I became so much better at honoring others' opinions than forming my own. And goodness, I'm a walking bomb defuser. You know when people at work melt down? Flip their desks? I'm on vacation when that happens. I'm a quelling force.

One evening during my teenage years, I was in the kitchen with my parents cleaning up after dinner. The radio was on, and my mother turned to me and said, "You like this sort of music?" in a tone that made clear she did not. And I was stunned. Really? Am I responsible for the music played by the station that happened to be on the radio that happened to be on? In the early 80s? Am I supposed to defend the song, my generation?

She obviously wanted a fight but by then I could recognize such an obvious trap. I imagine we all learned early how to become less of a target around her. Do not offer an opinion, do not share your feelings. Nod a lot. I can't remember what song it was. If I did like it, there's a good chance I felt wrong about that and carried that around. I didn't agree with her on a lot of things — she could be completely irrational sometimes — but I knew to keep my silence. I didn't know how to feel. I didn't want to agree with my mother about everything, or anything, for that matter. But I didn't want to fight about it, either.

Worried as I am about disagreement, I don't know how to form opinions on the fly. I'm shocked when I watch TV with friends and they're able to pick apart the episode even before the credits roll. They have fully developed opinions on the story arcs, how it all fits in the canon. Meanwhile I was just watching the show. I'm getting better, but I can't always experience and analyze at the same time. Lots of people say you really shouldn't, some others say you really can't — they are different brain processes. But in any case, I have to feel very strongly one way or another to start taking notes.

Similarly, after a movie, I dread the inevitable postmortem over coffee and cake. Really? Already? Do we have to talk about themes and the director's vision? I can't turn it around that quick. Partly because of this history, I can't comfortably proceed unless I know how you want me to respond. But I also just enjoy watching movies in the theater. I love the whole sensory experience: did the popcorn have real butter? Was it a cool reprieve on a particularly hot summer day? I have a good time almost every time I go to "the movies" but you want to talk about "the film?" Ugh. It'll be anywhere from hours to weeks before I figure that out. But sure, let's get a drink and you can save me the trouble. And by all means, monologue about it, because that's my favorite.

I took a film appreciation class in college, and we had to view a series of movies on campus. One was *Shane*, and I remember rather innocently saying that it was one of my father's favorite movies. I went with some classmates to watch it, and when the lights came on, my friend stood and said, "Your father liked that movie?" really loud in the crowd of attendees. I was mortified. I'd assumed it was a good movie, until that moment, when I learned that it wasn't. And then, what? Was I supposed to defend him? How could I? Her opinion seemed so much more correct than mine. After the class lecture on it, my friend exonerated my dad by acknowledging that the film was indeed better than she thought at first, but of course she said it privately.

It's rare for me to not to feel wrong about my take on something, especially when someone feels very strongly about theirs, which is of course to say they are louder about it. The more passionate they are, the more correct they seem to be. And I can't dredge up the necessary fire to defend most things, because I know exactly where the conversation will end up. It will feel just like a fight. And in the end, the other person will think a little less of me. And so will I, because I have no courage in my convictions.

There are times I'm not hiding my opinion at all. I don't know how to feel about a given thing, because I don't yet know how *you* feel about it. Once I know that, I'll know how to navigate, how to take care of you. It's only later that I can pull it all apart, figure out where I belong. Everyone knows the feeling of regret after not saying the perfect thing, which one usually figures out anywhere from seconds to minutes after the conversation took place. It takes me as much as a week or more. This book exists because of all the things I wish I'd thought of sooner or had the courage to say in the moment.

Those who are Extremely Opinionated have locked into a power position socially, and that leads inevitably, it seems, to *actual* power. What do you say to the virulent racist? How do you respond to someone with that much anger and fear driving them? It makes everything worse that they are winning the fight because we have no real tools in the face of it.

They are in charge in the family, in the acting school, in Congress. The loudest person will almost always end up at the center of a group of people like me, who are dedicated to — even dependent on — keeping the volume down. Reflexively agreeing just to keep the peace, we offer almost no resistance, even though we can tell it's an act. And those people, having created a persona around being The One Most Likely to Pontificate, paint themselves into a corner. Their opinions start to feel arbitrary, if not completely fabricated. Most of these folks are just making shit up, driven by their own demons to Be Heard No Matter What. They've long forgotten, if they ever cared, that they should also make sense, be kind, allow that others be afforded the same thing they are demanding for themselves.

I don't wear t-shirts in support of any musician or band. I have no bumper stickers on my car. I am very, very careful about debatable issues. I'm secretly quite passionate about politics, but I generally don't share those views. Show me someone who has been swayed from their view by a debate — other than me, I mean, and for better reasons than mine — and I might reconsider. It's just noise, and no one is listening. Those pundits aren't convincing anyone new. They're just screeching to the choir.

Love makes you vulnerable, we already know that. But I got some wires crossed. When I offer you something I love, something poignant or funny or interesting, I can't help but feel like I've shown you a little piece of myself. I think this is the crux of it, really: we share a piece of knowledge about ourselves every time we send a link or share an opinion.

There are ways to do this — to differ on something and still take decent care of the person who has, to one degree or another, made themselves vulnerable to you. But of course, thanks to my screamy mom, I don't think it's possible to strongly disagree with anyone and still be loved and respected by them. I feel at risk when I fight with you, when I share something I care about. And that sounds extreme, but we all know how easily opinions can change about actual people, that it happens all the time. Wars are fought over differences of opinion, bombs are dropped. People drive their car into groups of protestors because they disagree with them. This isn't a small thing, it's the only thing.

I write things down because I need time to put my thoughts together, to work on the whys and wherefores. And I'm more comfortable sharing my feelings on paper and on stage, where I can make my case in a way that ensures you'll listen until I'm done. No one can interrupt with a pointed finger and five-dollar words and a raised goddamned voice. When I'm lucky, and if I'm careful, I can maybe make myself understood without hurting anyone. Then, and I'm working on being okay with this, you may agree or disagree.

Non-Starter

I BOUGHT SOURDOUGH STARTER a couple of months ago, and I've been wondering why ever since. It's not like I need another mouth to feed. I was caught up in the fantasy of being someone who bakes sourdough bread from scratch. I am beset by ideas like this one, notions that seem to fill in the picture of the person I want to be, or wish I were. This happens to me all the time and it turns out I am never that person.

Feeding the sourdough starter isn't hard. It's laughably easy, in fact. But I still resent the pressure. As much as I want to be someone who takes time to perfect bread making techniques and has the patience to wait out the multiple proofing sessions, someone who can eat bread without worrying about a blood sugar spike, I'm just not. But starter is very seductive. Something about its long history, its simplicity, the fact that it exists at all. It's *sorcery*. It plucks wild yeast from the air! I want to be a part of that.

I used to feel the same passion for knitting, but whatever fire it lit within me is now decidedly banked. The yarn, at least, can sit there. The starter requires more of me. I need to feed it regularly, and I know I won't do right by it. But I can't throw it away, this living thing, this bubbling pile of potential. Who do I think I am?

I know that not everyone can do everything. We all have things we're good at, things that interest us, but most people can at least identify the things they are most likely to actually do. I'm terrible at that. I want to be the person who does _____, but I rarely consider what being good at _____ will require of me. Certainly not in the store, not at the moment of clicking "place order." I get so caught up in the ideal version of me.

If I spend too much time at a garden center, for example, I'll get inspired to redesign my entire front yard. These feelings are so seductive in the moment that I will fill the car with multiple flats of perennials and many cubic feet of soil, only to find upon arriving at home that the urge will have already disappeared. I'll feel pressured and frustrated, and it will take ages, and I'll resent the watering schedule, and eventually the yard will look exactly like it does now. Neglected.

I've never stopped wondering what I could be good at. My artist parents made my sisters and I believe we would all excel at something special of our own. But they didn't help us to identify a unique skill or encourage a particular talent. They failed to feed the starter, I suppose.

I commenced the search, but that thing never revealed itself no matter what I bought or convinced myself I might be good at. Poised to buy all the supplies for my latest aspirational hobby, maybe all I really needed was someone to step in and say, "This isn't it." Maybe not. Maybe I do need to learn the lesson over and over.

It's no mystery why I mostly chose domestic crafts and arts, the kinds of things you can fail at privately. I do well enough at baking and cooking, but it's because I so carefully select dishes that are both impressive and easy. It's the same with knitted gifts. I want to be the one who can create beautiful, tasty, useful things; I want to grow a beautiful garden. But I don't much want to get up off the couch.

I must confront what seems to be an essential laziness on my part. And I do think that's part of it, beyond a lack of guidance growing up. Shouldn't I *want* to expend energy on something that really turns my crank? Wouldn't the right thing move me? I know my depression and a lack of self-worth factors in, but it's the hand I've drawn. What excites me? What do I want to work on? It's weird when the answer is nothing, but I sure as hell haven't found it yet. Time is ticking.

Starter mostly makes itself. Water and flour, given time, will become something completely unique. It's a relationship, a healthful codependency. All you have to do is feed it.

Cold Hard World

I PURSUED ACTING IN high school, but despite getting high marks in my theater and acting classes, I didn't get cast in any plays. It was a small program, and the director also taught my acting classes, so there was a disconnect that confounded me. It could have been a harbinger of things to come, but I think it was mostly about the usual bullshit. I mean, it wasn't wrong for me to think my success in class would naturally progress to landing roles, that her knowledge of what I was capable of might inform her casting decisions.

Auditions for the plays and musicals were set up much like they are depicted in the movies — in the cavernous theater, four people lined up to watch from the darkness beyond the stage — no allowances for the fact that this was the first time we were doing this. And casting was very much like it would be from then on, by which I mean seemingly based on Things Besides Talent.

I wasn't admitted to the drama club either, another impenetrable space, although it was also run by the teacher who awarded me top marks in class. There was a big gathering so the club leaders could announce the names of the new crop of members, building pointless suspense like it was an awards show. The student leader garbled the last name, and I honestly thought it might have been mine. I approached her to confirm. "Was that my name?" I asked.

I still think about what my face must have looked like when she said "no." To this day, I don't know why they were so committed to excluding interested people.

It's a wonder I made it through any of this with dreams intact. But we're told over and over to never give up, and about how the external lack of faith in one's abilities is what drove so very many people to the top. *I'll show you*, I thought. *Just you wait.*

So I took the next class, challenged myself in scenes, attended every play. After one of those performances, I cried in the car the whole way home, much to my father's silent discomfort. I even went to my teacher's off-off-Broadway solo show, for pity's sake. Hers was the only game in town, what choice did I have? Eventually, I did get a role in the chorus of *Bye Bye Birdie*, during which I mouthed rather than sang the words and got yelled at along with everyone else by the musical director, a notorious asshole. It felt "real," this was the big time, or at least, it was just like the big time. He's yelling at us about our commitment levels! How exciting!

Looking back, I realize that I did have faith in my abilities, I just have no idea where that came from. The usual mixed messages were certainly external — my mother, my teachers — but also within me there existed both a total lack of confidence in myself and a strong belief in my talents. I know now to add my mental illness into the mix, but I honestly don't know how I came to think I was both shit and also *the* shit. I played out that internal tug of war for literal decades. You gotta believe, right? But I had no real proof. There weren't opportunities for me to try, no one willing to let me fail, to help me learn and get better. We were expected to arrive fully formed even though we were in high school. There was no space for less than perfect during the most gangly, awkward, and insecure time of our lives. The winners were the outliers: the prettiest, the most confident. There was no room for us regular folks.

A college friend of mine went on to teach high school theater and she once mentioned how difficult it is to find plays that accommodate all the kids who show up to auditions. That was her minimum requirement. I know some of you are thinking, "Life is hard," right now. If this sounds like participation trophy stuff, go back and read this again. It's just the participation part. Let more people be a part of more things, let them enter spaces they're usually not welcomed into. And would it hurt if we were a little more careful with the hearts and souls of adolescents? For some, rejection cuts a little deeper at that age, before we're more secure with ourselves, less driven by hormones and scared of mean girls. There was no earthly reason they couldn't have made that space larger. Denying kids the chance to try things out, to fail, is to cut out a group of dedicated, excited people that might make something richer and more interesting.

In the end, I eschewed it all and entered a college program that was entirely wrong for me, immediately failed a class (Molecular and Cellular Biology, in my defense), and spent the rest of my time slowly wending my way back to the arts. At the end of my sophomore year, I was cast as Mrs. Drudge in Tom Stoppard's *The Real Inspector Hound*. It was the best time I could have imagined, and it also probably ruined my life. It was vindication; it felt like everything had slotted into place. I was insufferable. For good or ill — no, for good *and* ill — I reoriented my path, and I chased that Mrs. Drudge high for twenty-odd years. Twenty odd years.

Stage Two:

Carcinojenny

Believe

MY HUSBAND WAS FORTY-ONE when he was diagnosed with colon cancer. The doctors were optimistic. Mark was young and strong, and they didn't have to be gentle with him in terms of treatment. It was a serious case and they treated it that way, but they didn't have to tread carefully because of his age or other illnesses. It was the best possible scenario, they told us. I think they were hopeful.

And so were we, initially. But hope and denial can look exactly the same. As time went on, it became clear he couldn't possibly survive. I remember distinctly the day the doctor sat us down and explained that Mark's cancer was incurable, and though he couldn't have been more direct, we ... still didn't get it.

The cancer survivor positivity movement is huge. It's a veritable flood of messages about the curative properties of thinking good thoughts, the power of prayer, and the miracles of modern medicine. Over and over, we heard the same stories about how a patient's doctors had all lost hope, but so-and-so proved them wrong.

It doesn't help that humans tend to do just this, selectively accepting only what supports our innermost wishes. Amidst all of this, for example, I was still hoping to have a creative career, even if the cancer had firmly put a pin in that plan. Regardless, the

odds were not in my favor. And I can't tell you how many times
people bring up that one actress who didn't start acting till she
was in her sixties. One person's unlikely success story is a case
against pursuing acting at my age, but we all want to believe we're
the exception. And eventually, we believe it, because otherwise
we'll have to face the wasted time and money and emotional
investment.

But the systems aren't exactly set up for us to quit either. We left
that meeting with the doctor with new prescriptions and a new
plan of attack (think: a different agent, a new set of headshots). It
wasn't the last time the doctor tried to get through to us. About
a year later the same one tried to convince me to convince Mark
that there was nothing more to be done. We were stubborn, he was
frustrated, and I was furious that he was putting it on me. I didn't
know how to face Mark's faith without mirroring it. I didn't know
how to be the person to say that all our effort was for nothing. We'd
worked so hard for so long; he'd had endured so much. In the end,
it was about sunk costs as much as it was anything else. But you
can do everything you're supposed to do, everything the experts
tell you to do, and still fail.

In the very, very bitter end, with an unconquerable infection in
play and the new tumor taking over, Mark agreed to the hospice
plan. He could go home, they said. He could be made comfortable
and pain free, and he could say his goodbyes. He was in the ICU at
that point, and right after he signed the papers, they began turning
off all the machines, one at a time, pulling meds, and so on. It was
deeply scary and surreal, never mind that it made perfect sense.
They weren't particularly gentle about it, but it wasn't heartless.

They were at work, and this was their job. It was just the next thing they had to do that day.

We'd made the decision too late. Mark was transferred to a different room — ICU beds are for ICU patients, after all — while the hospice folks began to implement a plan so he could come home. The new room was on a noisy hall with a nurse-to-patient ratio we were not accustomed to. The difference was stark. When one of the hospice team came to visit, she greeted Mark and then pulled me aside to ask me if I'd called his mom yet. I was shocked, of course. "You should," she said. I'll always be grateful to her. I called. His mother arrived the next day, along with his sister and brother, and he died later that night.

Subway

ONE DAY, AS WE returned to our apartment from the oncologist's office, Mark said, out of the blue, "I guess I feel like a subway." He was not a man given to this kind of poetic self-assessment, and I was desperate to understand.

He was in the middle of a six-week-long Monday-to-Friday chemo course. The pump he carried with him all week had been disconnected. We were maybe a couple of months into the cancer ride, and still reeling from the shock of it.

Well, I can only guess. I was a robot then. I've never known a more productive period, in terms of just getting things done. You wouldn't believe it if you saw it in action. I'm great at funerals; there will never be a glass that needs to be filled or a casserole heated or a floor vacuumed, because I will have taken care of it. That's Robot Jenny, and she's great to have around. Sure, I'm not really feeling my feelings, but that's the best part.

Mark had already had the first surgery to remove a mass in his colon. It was to have been a fairly routine procedure, where they remove the section of the colon with the mass, along with a few inches on either side, to make sure the margins are clear. Sew it up and off you go. In Mark's case, there was some trepidation — results were iffy on whether the mass was benign or precancerous.

The surgery revealed the mass to be huge and definitely cancer. It was no longer contained in the colon but had made its way through the colon wall itself. In fact, it was dangerously close to the rectum, which complicated things a great deal. (Ahem, schedule that colonoscopy.)

While he was still on the operating table, the doctor presented me with our limited options. We decided he would remove as much of the cancer as he could and put in a temporary colostomy, so that Mark could be in on the decisions that had to be made regarding the rest of his treatment. We could do another surgery in a few days, to make the temporary thing permanent and close all the openings that needed to be closed. Or we could take some time to hammer at the growth with radiation and chemo, and then see if it wasn't possible to reconnect all the parts and restore functionality to his colon. This was the first of many weird forks in the cancer road, and there's no way to know if the other path might have been better or worse. If we'd just taken it all out right then and let radiation and chemo have its day, perhaps he wouldn't have been fighting it more than three years later. Perhaps he wouldn't have gotten the blood clot or the pulmonary embolism. Or maybe the cancer wouldn't have spread to his bladder, and he wouldn't have had to have that removed and a new one built with yet more of his beleaguered colon. Maybe he wouldn't have had the aneurysm, or the infection he couldn't get rid of, and maybe the cancer wouldn't have returned to his pelvic wall.

It's impossible to know. We just listened to the doctors, chose a path, and tried not to look back.

People told me, "I could never do what you're doing," but you don't get a choice. It's true that some people do fall apart, hide under the bed, whatever, but most step up. With no crystal ball, you do the thing that makes the most sense. Don't look at the mountain; just take the next step.

Now, I see that this period was a kind of practice for future events. Looking forward to a day when this process or that treatment would be over, then being forced to reset the plan and push back the deadlines. It trained me for things like waiting for job offers and global pandemics.

There was an extremely short-lived cancer awareness ad campaign during this time, in which high-profile survivors talked about how cancer couldn't defeat them because they were so determined that it not. One woman (who has since died from cancer) stared straight into the camera and said, "I refuse to let cancer beat me." I've never been so deeply offended in my life.

We joked about it. "Did you remember to refuse, hon?"

"Oh, yeah," Mark would say. "I gotta remember to do that."

It was baffling. Perhaps lofty tones and a steely gaze were her secret weapons. I guess all we had to do was decline cancer's invitation in no uncertain terms. It seems unlikely that no one in that brainstorming session had a connection to an actual cancer patient, but the evidence said otherwise.

It was frustrating for Mark to tell people good news about some test results only for them to say things like, "Just goes to show you, prayer works." He hung up the phone one time muttering, "I'm busting my ass over here."

He deserved some credit, I think, for following all the protocols. A few points to medical science, not to mention his team of healthcare professionals, and sure, some to me, his live-in nurse.

On the flip side, if results weren't what we were hoping for, it would be because "they didn't pray hard enough."

One time I mentioned to my father's wife that Mark's oncologist was pleased and surprised with his progress, and she responded, "Hasn't he heard about the power of prayer?"

He's an oncologist. I'm pretty sure he's got a more complicated relationship with the Lord than you seem to. On another occasion, when I wasn't sufficiently hopeful, she asked, "Jenny, *where* is your *faith*?" as if a) anyone's wouldn't be shaken after what Mark and I had been through, and b) I'd had any to begin with.

I'm not saying you *shouldn't* refuse to die from cancer. Pray if you want to, and think positively if you can manage it, but also take your medicine. Try to keep from thinking about the fact that all of that only works some of the time. There are a million microscopic variables at work. It's luck. Same as with everything. Nothing is guaranteed. Nothing ever is.

If I never hear the phrase "courageous battle with cancer" again, it will be too soon. There is no such thing as a cowardly fight with cancer. And what's with all the fighting talk, anyway? It suggests that there is a knowable path to winning. If it doesn't work, what? It's the patient's fault, he wasn't fighting hard enough — is that it? Go to hell. I'm certainly not the first to point this out, but we've cloaked the cancer patient's experience so thoroughly in language about combat that I can't think of any other words, and by now it should be clear how much I like to describe things with words. The problem is that the language is made for the winners, the survivors. Yes, Mark lost his so-called fight with cancer, but cancer never really wins. It's a terrible, terrible draw.

When I asked Mark if he minded me writing about this, he had no objections. Hundreds of people knew his personal business, after all. In the hospital, you really do become just a thing — an engine with mechanical trouble. Which is not to say they don't treat you well, but it's best if you can let go of things like modesty and embarrassment. They won't serve you. If you've ever spoken to a woman who'd very recently given birth, you'll know what I mean. They'll tell you all of it, from the look of the mucus plug to the size of the poop that came out while they were bearing down, things you know they would never otherwise volunteer. But in a hospital, it's entirely clinical, all business.

When I'd stub my toe or get a paper cut, I would play it up for Mark. "WHY ME?" I'd shout at the heavens. "I HAVE THE WORST LUCK!"

It's true Mark and I were in it together, but we lived in two different worlds. I had no idea what it was like to have cancer, and he had no idea what it was like to be a cancer patient's caregiver. For what it's worth, I don't think I could do what Mark did, certainly not with the grace with which he did it. And I do wonder how he'd have been in my shoes, juggling the patient, the job, the house, the pets, the insurance companies. I suppose I should take my own advice and trust that we could do what the other did because there would be no choice. But insight into how he felt was so important to me. I wanted to be there for him. And I certainly didn't expect for him to feel like a subway.

So, when he said that, my mind just took off. Perhaps he felt like he was in the dark, hurtling towards an unknown destination .... Or maybe that there were passengers aboard his train — insidious little cells that wouldn't get off but just sat there, multiplying. I repeated it back to him, "You feel like a subway?"

"Yeah," he said. "Like, turkey and cheese, with mustard and pickles. No mayo."

"Ohhhhh. From Subway. OK. On it."

Bit Part: Untouchable

FOR A SICK PERSON to get well, they need fresh air, uninterrupted sleep, a germ-free environment, and quality food. None of that is available in a hospital.

You're there because you are, essentially, malfunctioning, and you're stripped of everything you usually disguise yourself with. You can have no secrets, about anything, right down to how much you just peed. But on the other hand, you have a vast number of people who will treat that machine, your body, with more tenderness and concern than most people have known since they were toddlers. The dissonance can be something of a mindfuck.

We would go it alone for as long as we could, but eventually, we'd hit a wall. Mark wasn't improving, or I was anxious about what I could reasonably provide at home, and we'd both be relieved when he was admitted to the hospital again. But then, tired of the routine, exhausted by the staff's constant vigilance, we'd be just as anxious to get back home.

This was the pattern for almost four years.

Carcinojenny

IN THE RUN-UP TO Mark's first surgery, we spread the word to family and a few friends. I explained over coffee or after a show that they'd detected a mass in his colon and were going to go in, resect the bowel, and close him up. We were optimistic; early biopsies cautiously suggested no malignancy. One friend asked how we'd known to investigate, and I told her there'd been some symptoms. And she said, immediately, "And of course you made him go to the doctor," like she was finishing the sentence for me.

I've thought about it a lot. Because I begged him to go — so, so many times. We talked about it, I reasoned, he agreed, but then he wouldn't do anything. It's not especially surprising. People don't generally rush to do others' bidding in life. And while I hoped for more from my own husband, the one who regularly said things like, "I'd do anything for you," I didn't have a successful history here. Stomping up to my bedroom and slamming the door never got me a single thing growing up. Yelling louder than my mom was a physical impossibility. My particular history made it even less likely that I would insist, whatever that might have looked like.

I wanted him to go because obviously something was wrong — something, to be fair, we couldn't fathom the extent of. We hadn't yet reached the age when strange symptoms cause immediate alarm. Looking back, he may have truly thought it was up to me to do this. I did so much of this kind of labor — bill paying, gift giving, list making — that maybe he thought I'd also take care of this. But he'd butted up against a war wound. I wanted to matter enough, for him to do the right thing because I asked. I couldn't know I held his life in my hands.

While many things could have been causing his symptoms, he was, I think, deeply afraid that it was exactly what they would eventually find. Early detection is a huge part of surviving cancer. And the longer he waited, the more danger he was putting both of us in.

I'd do anything for you. Except call the doctor's office.

I fear I've unconsciously replicated this dynamic in other areas of my life. A large part of my current job entails getting my boss to his next meeting on time. The difficulty of this is a running joke I can usually join in on — I have a very high threshold, obviously. No matter how important the meeting, or how difficult it was to schedule, it doesn't always work. People stop him on the way and conversations run long. Some days I feel, irrationally, like crying. *You're making so much more work for me.* It falls to me to clean up the mess and re-shuffle meetings because it's my job and he's a grown man who makes his own decisions. I can clear, pave, and light the path, but he has to walk it. I am not in charge here.

Mark's expectation that I would make that appointment is no more fair than me obsessing over why I didn't. It wasn't my job to do that, though of course I feel responsible. How else could I possibly feel?

You might be thinking, "You can't make someone do what they don't want to do." And I hear that. Except ... yes, you can. When it matters, of course you can. After years of this tug-of-war, Mark finally confessed to what he'd been keeping from me — there was blood in his stool. Do you know what I did? I picked up the phone and made an appointment. And then he went. Simple.

So yes, of course I made him go to the doctor.

Patience Zero

MARK'S BIGGEST COMPLAINTS WERE about the smallest things. I wouldn't have blamed him for railing at the heavens about his plight, but he never did. He never asked, "Why me?" Instead, he complained about things so small, it was occasionally infuriating.

Once, I handed him a new bottle of Tylenol, and he said, "This isn't the fast-acting one," fully expecting me to right this wrong. I mean, for real? He wanted me to go back to the drug store and return with faster acting pills? By which time his headache would have been gone. Isn't fast-acting relative here? Aren't all the OTC pain relievers in the fast-acting business? Why do they even make a separate line of these? Who would choose the slower acting one? Me, that's who.

Mark found the smell of the canned cat food I gave to our cat to be simply more than he could bear and told me so every single damn time he was in whiffing distance of the stuff. Louise was an insulin-dependent diabetic cat, a condition that was discovered shortly after Mark's cancer diagnosis. That all three of us were still alive was a damn miracle.

I know he was just stuck for fixable things to complain about, but I can't help how cat food smells. I was the one who regularly cleaned out his colostomy bag, if we're talking about strong odors no one can do anything about.

When you're as sick as Mark was, your focus turns entirely inward, which is normal and as it should be. As the caregiver, I was also focused on him, but he couldn't put me in the mix. Which surprised us both, I think, because it was so unlike his regular self.

I once found a coveted parking spot near the entrance to the oncologist's office, and he wondered aloud and with some irritation why I didn't just go to the parking structure.

"Because if I did, I'd have to leave you in the car, go downstairs, over to the doctor's building, go upstairs to the office, borrow a wheelchair, bring it back to the car, take you over to the office and then repeat that in reverse at the end. Also, we don't have to pay to park here."

He felt terrible, and I was sorry for being a jerk about it, but how had he missed all that effort?

People would say, "How nice, your nurse is your wife." But he never argued with nurses the way he did with me. Once, he pushed my hands away when I was changing his dressing and I had to count to a million.

When I tried to talk to him about how he might go benefit from antidepressants, or how important it was that he eat more, it was like so much buzzing in his ears. One day at the hospital, after the social worker left his room, he said to me, as if the subject had never come up, "We're going to try some antidepressants. She thinks it would be a good idea."

Later *that same day*, his sister spent some time with him and Mark said to me afterwards, "You know, Jen, I really need to push myself to eat more. You gotta feed the machine."

And I said, "Yeah, you know? You're right."

I was also taking care of a houseful of pets. Two dogs and the cat, and then the extra cat, and then one dog died, and the yard cats showed up, and then the other dog died, and so on. Pet care is consuming and expensive even when nothing else is going on. But in the middle of everything, Yard Kitty, the yard kitty, started behaving strangely. She was sluggish, and not as interested in her food. I eventually discovered a large abscess in the long hair on her chin. It was a Saturday night, and since waiting till Monday seemed risky, I took her to the Emergency Vet Clinic.

Now, I rarely played the cancer card. For the first couple of years, it didn't come up at all. Our business was just that, and telling random people about it would do nothing at all. But when the vet tech brought me the $1200 estimate to essentially pop a zit, I hit my limit.

"Look," I said, "my husband has cancer, we're in the middle of chemo treatments, and this cat's name is *Yard Kitty*. I don't know who she belongs to, and I can tell you right now, I don't have $1200 to lance this boil."

The tech excused herself and came back with a new plan. It was still pricey — emergency vets aren't saints — but they cut the cost in half, assured of my willingness to keep her in the house and handle the follow-up care.

Early the next morning, while Mark was sleeping, I picked Yard Kitty up at the vet and put her our extra room. This was the room where Mark's mother, who was coincidentally arriving that day and also allergic to cats, was supposed to stay. And no, Yard Kitty had never seen a litter box before. She had a drain thing in her chin, medications she flatly refused to take, and frankly, I was teetering on an edge.

Meanwhile, our big dog was tippy tapping all over the place, all excited about the new guest, and making a fuss. That woke Mark, who naturally asked what was going on.

"She's just excited because Yard Kitty is in the house."

And Mark said, "She's in the *house*?"

I sort of lost it. It had been a long night. I mean it, what were my options? I said to him, through clenched teeth, "I don't know what to tell you, Mark. This is why you love me!"

And then I left to go get his mother from the airport. She was fine with taking the couch. It was way more comfortable than that futon. And anyway, Yard Kitty had peed on the futon.

The Ornamental Penis

ONCE HE WAS DIAGNOSED, Mark's illness lasted three years, ten months, and nine days. Through it all, we only called 9-1-1 once.

It was about three or four in the morning, and I was to wake up in just a couple of hours to bring Mark's mother, Mary, to the airport after a week-long visit. I had, only a few hours earlier, returned from a weekend trip to a friend's wedding, which I could comfortably attend only because his mom had been there to stay with Mark. The plan had gone off without a hitch. I was not fully aware that Mark had gotten up to go to the bathroom, but I felt him lie back down next to me and heard him say, "Honey, wake up, I'm bleeding."

I didn't panic right away. It was not the first emergency we'd faced, and by that point, we'd had some very scary moments. He gestured vaguely toward the bathroom, and I shuffled off, only to find a veritable river of blood. It was *everywhere*. My first instinct was to clean it up, so I could spare my mother-in-law the shock of seeing it. But I abandoned that plan as soon as it formed — there was so much. Something was obviously terribly wrong. I went back to the bedroom and called 9-1-1, woke Mary up, and we were off to the ER.

When a permanent colostomy is placed, your rectum is removed, and they sew your anus closed. A small opening is left, which should eventually close on its own, once the surgical drainage and whatnot is done. Mark's opening never fully closed. So, if you're wondering, and you probably are, where the blood was coming from, he had an aneurysm in his interior iliac artery, and the blood escaped through that opening. Had it healed as it should have, he would have bled to death before we knew anything serious was wrong.

After a week in the ICU, and a couple of other dramatic bleeding episodes, Mark appeared to be getting better. Scans were inconclusive, since Mark's insides didn't look anything like a regular person's would, but after all he'd been through, doctors were reluctant to choose surgical means to figure it out. He sat up in a chair for a few hours, but when he was moved back to the bed, he started bleeding again, the most serious episode yet. He just sat in a pool of his own blood. I held his hand while a team of six nurses worked on him, directed by a woman named Judy. Two or three bags of blood were hung over the bed with these bulbs in the line, and they would just keep squeezing those bulbs, essentially pumping blood into his body as quickly as it was escaping, and changing the bags out as needed. They surrounded the bed, and honestly, they were all so calmly efficient, you'd never have known they were saving his life. Judy never broke a sweat, and neither did Mark, to his credit. He was calm and curious throughout, and I described what was going on. They got him stabilized, and in the wee hours of the morning, a vascular surgeon found and closed a hole in his artery through magical non-surgical means. I watched the procedure on a monitor.

ICU nurses usually had two patients each, but that night he had a dedicated nurse. She sat outside his room and watched him through a window while Mark's mother and I dozed in reclining chairs. I woke at one point when the nurse came in to tuck warmed blankets around us both, and it still makes me cry to think about it. There's no one like an ICU nurse.

When we'd first been admitted to the hospital for this episode, we were met there after an hour or so by his oncologist, a very kind man who clearly never got the memo about emotional detachment being the best course of action with your patients. Good test results always came with a hug, and now that I think about it, bad test results did, too. Now, by this point in the cancer journey, Mark's bladder had been removed and replaced with a pouch made from a portion of his small intestine. It was accessed by a catheter through a hole roughly where his navel used to be. So, his penis wasn't attached to anything on the inside, but he felt the need to make a full report to the doctor. In case you're wondering what kind of patient he was, it was here that Mark rather casually said, "Doc, there's blood also coming out of my penis. I mean, I know it's just ornamental at this point ...."

The doctor turned away to hide a smile, and it made Mark's day. I don't think there are many men who could calmly refer to their penis as ornamental, not even to make the doctor laugh.

After another week or so of recovery, and a total of twelve bags of blood, we were back home. He'd live another sixteen months.

Bit Part: Help

WHILE MARK WAS SICK, I had so many offers of help, I thought I'd have to make up things for people to do. Everyone was so well-meaning and loving, and I felt it, I did. But telling people how to help us also became just another thing I had to do. I know I sound like an asshole, but I think people often want to feel as though they've been helpful and that is not always the same as being helpful. We are all guilty of this sometimes; it isn't a conscious thing. We chase the reward, that good feeling.

After our mom's funeral, my sisters and I raced back to the house from the gravesite to clean up before the guests came over, but one of them waltzed in right behind us and started doing the dishes. We were horrified. "NO, please, don't!" we all said, because we're cut from the same cloth. She would not be moved. And we were upset and angry and embarrassed and, finally, grateful. It was nice not to have to do the dishes; it was help we needed. But it was so hard for us to let someone lift that burden.

I'm part of my own equation. Rationally, I know needing help isn't a bad thing. But it feels like a strike against me. During Mark's illness, I couldn't let people in. I was invested in maintaining an illusion of competency. But also, my hands were full, and his life was on the line. What part of that could I comfortably job out?

Help comes in so many forms. For the most part, people offer what they would want for themselves, so it's good information if you take notes. Massages were a hot ticket item, but I have a body disorder. I couldn't imagine literally laying myself bare like that. I mean, I think I could have gotten there eventually, but it would have taken a lot of work, and I didn't have the time. I also felt, strongly, that my tension was holding me up. If I relaxed at all, I was sure I'd fall apart.

The Newlywid

THE AFTERMATH OF MARK'S death was a blur. I was not in my body, really, which is saying something considering how not in my body I am on a regular day. But I'd committed to a certain persona, one who was most assuredly Not Falling Apart, and you have to act the part you've been cast in. You must honor the contract.

Whether you do a good job or not is for the critics, but I think I did an okay job. It's like you're flying a plane, say, and you have all this responsibility and concern, all these buttons and dials to monitor, and you're in charge of all of it going just so. There are people depending on you to do this. And sure, some of the knobs have come off, and a few needles are in the red zone, but you're still managing. You know you can keep going.

Then someone else pushes the eject button.

It's jarring. You don't need to care about any of the things that consumed you just moments before. You don't have to do anything at all except float to the ground, only vaguely curious about a parachute.

My first thought after Mark died was, "Who will love me now?" and I was ashamed of that. But I know myself; I'm not easy to find. And he had such a big heart, I counted on him to fill in the blanks, all the ways I couldn't see — let alone love — myself. It's a lot to ask of anyone, and it's a lot to do without.

In the beginning I thought, "Gosh, I hope I don't have to re-remember that he's gone every morning." Like in all those movies where the lonely spouse wakes up, and we watch as slowly the reality of their miserable existence descends. They roll over to see the empty space beside them, and then, ever so gently — and with the back of the hand only, for some reason — they caress the pillow. Those scenes are why I took to sleeping diagonally across the bed from the start. Even when he was in the hospital, I'd sleep like a starfish so when I woke up there was no doubt I was alone in the bed.

Even when we were in the bed together, incidental touching wasn't really allowed. He was in so much discomfort from various wounds: recent surgeries, the infection, scars, his poor bottom. Once, I accidentally spooned him in my sleep and caused him excruciating pain.

On my own for the first time in more than twenty years, and recently laid off from my job, I remember proudly telling my therapist that I'd started to set the alarm clock for eight hours from whatever time I was going to bed. Look at me finally getting a decent night's sleep. When she very reasonably asked why I bothered to set the alarm at all, I was stumped. I could only claim the minimum for myself.

Without Mark or a job, I didn't have anything to do. The vacuum that opened in my life after almost four years of relentless doing was so destabilizing, I immediately started to fill it up. I had to. Lots of widows have to go right back to work after their spouses die, and if I had been employed, a job would have filled the time, provided structure, eased me back into life. I would never have purposely stepped away from work to focus on myself or the grief, so I was grateful to have the space and freedom to do whatever I wanted, to decompress but also to devote myself to my own goals. But this period lasted much longer than was strictly therapeutic.

Right after someone dies, there's a flurry of focused attention from friends and loved ones. It's wonderful, really, but it inevitably ends, and you are alone. I was with Mark for twenty years, so I felt alone. And it's disorienting. People would ask what they could do, but well, there was nothing. I couldn't come up with stuff even when I needed help, but I had less to do now than ever before. There was such a small list of practicalities to tend to: feed the cats, do some grocery shopping. The big stuff — build a life, figure out what you want, pursue any goddamn thing for yourself — no one could help me with.

I didn't feel single, but I sure as hell felt alone. I was constantly aware that no one really knew where I was at any given time, that if I were abducted while running errands, say, no one would ever find me. I was also watching way too much procedural cop shows, in which 80% of the victims are single females, living alone, and who all seemed really nice.

Caregivers tend to ignore their own needs to take care of others, so they are notoriously endangered. There are lots of stories about people falling ill within weeks of their patient getting better or dying. I have a friend whose parents died within days of each other because her mom ignored a persistent pain while taking care of her sick husband.

I went to the doctor after Mark died and was diagnosed with Metabolic Derangement, the perfect name for it. It included hypothyroidism, high blood sugar, high cholesterol, an infection in my small intestine, and various vitamin deficiencies. I was angry my own body had betrayed me, of course, though I also don't know why I expected a body that I had spent so much time hating to still come through for me. I guess I thought it was the least it could do.

I kicked around that big house by myself with absolutely nothing that had to get done, trying to figure out how to put myself first. Each morning, I realized that because I was the only one drinking coffee, it felt like I was wasting a filter. I bought a pour-over thing with a reusable cloth insert, problem solved. Also a French press and a stovetop percolator thing, so I could make coffee in a bunch of ways, if anyone were to come over.

I joined Facebook a month or so before Mark died, and it ended up being the principal way I alleviated the concerns of my family and friends and sold the story of How Great I was Doing. I was unfailingly positive. It was early days for both the site and my widowhood, so there were a lot of posts like, "Doing the laundry!" Not all that interesting, but it was a great way to put others at ease about how things were going.

That relentless, possibly fake optimism is interesting to me, but I was also reporting on a lot of activity — essay shows, submissions, improv, short films, auditions, voiceovers. I was working as a personal assistant and doing a little freelance writing to make money. I was busier than I've given myself credit for. I wouldn't have remembered that if I hadn't written it down. Part of me wishes

I hadn't. It's less painful to think I failed because I didn't try than that I failed even though I did.

For a time, it felt like things were going well. I went to shows, I started a Newlywid blog, I took commercial acting classes. I was desperate to do creative things, but I also wanted something to report back to the concerned. The photos taken in the year after Mark died are perhaps the best evidence of how I was really doing. My smile was a strained rictus. "I am fine," it totally fails to say. I was a living version of that grimacing emoji.

Though I'd never joined any of the support groups offered to caregivers during Mark's illness — because who has the time — right after he died, I thought joining an online community might help. As a fairly young Newlywid, I was interested to find someone my age who'd already been through the death of a spouse, and I signed up to a forum with a straightforward-sounding name. I don't click on links to places like *soaringspirits.com* or *rainbowlove.sad*, I know that much about myself.

The beginning was fabulous — so many great people were here with me in this crappy boat! It was such a relief. I had a brief honeymoon period with the site, same as any social network, before it all fell apart.

At some point, doubts began to creep in as I realized how little I really had in common with them. There was, for example, a group for newly single parents. There was a Motorcycle Group, a Suicide Group, and the Second Time Around group, for those who'd been widowed more than once. It was overwhelming. And it seemed more and more that the thing that connected us wasn't remotely enough to hold us together.

Being with others who have similar experiences is good if that works for you. But commiseration has its limits. I may share someone's general feeling of surreality after losing a spouse, and I can perhaps guide you through some of the practical things one might have to deal with in the first few months. But that's about all. "I know just how you feel," is a fiction.

"Community of widows," was, for me, an oxymoron. And I know I sound like an asshole; I felt like one, too. But feeling alone in that group was hard, too hard. The central thing that bound us seemed to be that we were all alone in our pain; our losses were too individual to ever be fully understood by another person.

Maybe because of this, conversations seemed to barely skim along the surface of things. Were we really going to talk about when to take our rings off? The answer is when you feel like it. Can we do my questions now?

How do you handle the fact that your husband wouldn't go to the doctor for three years, despite your pleading and begging, and that he hid the scariest symptoms from you? Where are the other people who wasted years of their lives bumbling around, wondering what life was all about and when it would start? Anyone out there whose spouse wasn't a saint? What are you doing now that the one person who gave a shit about the ins and outs of your day isn't there anymore? Is anyone else furious? My anger shows no sign of letting up; quite the contrary. How do you deal with the fact that the world just doesn't agree that it owes you something for all this? I don't want quotes about how other people feel. Tell me your true feelings, and if you can't do that, by god, make it funny. You people are sinking this crappy boat.

I soon realized that hearing all these other heartbreaking stories of other peoples' losses was a very good way to not deal with my own.

Someone posted about how the first year as a widow is a piece of cake compared to the second and third years, and my panic was complete. And over the next day, on the widow forum, I went through, in very quick succession, what's known as the five stages of grief — except that in my case, step one was deleting my account.

Everyone grieves their own way. I know. *I know.*

I think we're all at different places on parallel paths, and that's the best we're going to get. You can wave at someone in the distance, walking at roughly the same pace, or give them a thumbs up, but you can't cross over. It has to be enough to know that others are out there.

Next, I joined a Young Widows and Widowers Group, another warm and welcoming online support resource that I nevertheless left within a few weeks. At the time Facebook didn't offer a choice for the widowed among their relationship options, and this was the main topic of discussion. I thought it was worth correcting, certainly. They finally added it, and I'm glad they did. Many people proudly self-branded, but I don't choose to show my relationship status at all, so nothing really changed for me. I mean, I get that it's a badge you want to wear. I noticed how quickly I would mention my widowhood when I met new people. It was information I really wanted them to know, not just that I'd been through something difficult, but that someone had loved me once.

Why do some people keep their couple selfies as their profile pictures? Why do people post photos of the engagement ring? What is a ring except proof that someone chose you? And how do you deal with it when that proof is gone?

Anyway, that's one reason people leave their rings on.

Bit Part: Holidays

IF THERE IS EVER a time to get some perspective on special occasions, it's when you or a loved one is in the hospital. It's Thanksgiving, you say? Well, he had an aneurysm, so if it's all the same to you, we'll have turkey another day.

This is, in the end, a day like any other. We imbue it with so much. And we buy into the relentless messaging from movies and commercials about home and hearth, and we spend a lot to get to that place, and take the family photo, and post the highlights on social media, and hope it all looks just right. I'm a cynic, obviously.

People are funny about the idea of spending the holidays alone. As with most things, they think about how they might feel in my shoes. I appreciate the concern, of course, but Thanksgiving is not better if I am among a sea of people I don't know, tacked on to the end of the table at someone else's family dinner. I like to be with my family, and if I can't be, then chances are I want to be alone.

If I can't be home for Christmas, then my second choice is to do exactly what I'm doing: sit here with a hot cuppa something, call my family, watch Doctor Who, knit a bit, and write stuff down.

This was seldom to be in the years after Mark died. I forgot that when you talk to other people, you need to be ready to satisfy them with your plans. And being by yourself is Not Acceptable, even if it's all you want for Christmas. It's like saying, "I didn't sleep with so-and-so," or "That wasn't me who farted." People believe what they want to believe.

Status Update

You know the passive-aggressive, bullshit thing people do on social media, where they make a general complaint about how "some people" have this or that offensive posting habit, or an irritating way of doing blah blah, pretending that this is just a general comment about others and not a direct criticism of some of their own followers? They're "just saying." It's transparent bullshit, and it's always irritating, but sometimes the barb really gets in there and it becomes something else.

In the aftermath of Mark's death, someone I follow posted about how "people on here" seem to like their pets more than they do people, and what a sad state of affairs that is. And of course, some of their friends — just being social, you understand — piled on to agree, posting comment after comment lamenting the loss of human interaction. On social media.

I know being provocative is the name of this game, and I get that some people need any attention they can get and don't care one way or the other if they are being honest or respectful or good friends. I even get that this right here is essentially a passive-aggressive post! But social media encourages the worst in people, the absolute worst. Honestly, it goes to everything I'm saying here — look how far people are willing to go, what they will say, how many human beings they are willing to hurt, just for the promise of more clicks and likes. Audience capture is everything. Some handle it responsibly; they have restraint and a strong moral center. Others destroy republics. The promise of an audience who might love you — or can provide a reasonable facsimile of love — can fuck with people's lives and mental health and sense of humanity.

This, I realize, was not as bad as all that. But it *hurt*. I refrained from commenting, but just barely. It was a road rage situation; I knew my reaction wasn't rational. I was a recent widow with four cats. I couldn't say anything that wouldn't come off as pathetic, and I was heavily invested in being Fine. Social media was how I got that message out. But I wrote and rewrote responses to that post in my head; I was obsessed for a time.

But it's impossible, even on a regular day, to convince a person with no particular connection to pets what that connection can mean. In seventh grade one of my teachers laughed out loud when I told her my cat died. "Sorry!" she said to my shocked face, "I thought you were kidding." It was a good lesson.

I had a wonderful support system during Mark's illness, people on call to do anything we needed, and they were there at the end, to help with anything I needed. It was a veritable tide of love and care and support. But that tide must recede; people went back to their lives, their own struggles and concerns. And I was left to myself, literally.

This is where the cats came in. There were, as I said, four. They would form a circle around me each evening when I settled on the couch. Calm, watchful, accepting, they didn't expect anything of me, and it was a balm. I fed and cared for them, but that was all they required. I didn't have to perform for them, put on my happy face, or otherwise spin stories about how surprisingly well I was doing. I could just be.

Pets are reliable. They give back and hold up their end of the bargain in ways we can't always count on people to do. They are always their little sweet selves, sometimes preternaturally tuned to what we need. And crucially, they never ever post passive-aggressive criticisms of people they know will see them.

Playing Possum

In my Newlywid days, I was mostly white knuckling it. I was on autopilot, filling my time by performing as much as possible, taking care of my acquired cat colony, and watching episodes of the new *Doctor Who*. A lot of it is a blur now, but I had a little money and some time to myself, so I was luckier than most. It could have been worse.

But there were moments that brought home just how alone I was, how little help I had. Dragging the garbage and recycling buckets out to the curb on collection day is a good example. You never saw anyone so bitter and self-pitying.

You know how in the police procedural TV shows, they say things like, "She wasn't in her right mind," or "The suspect can't recall how she got to the warehouse." It often feels like this is sheer fiction, just a plot device. Well, let me tell you about the night a juvenile possum got into my house, and instead of accepting that reality, I made up a whole story in my head so I wouldn't have to do anything about it.

I'd been watching a movie and surrounded, as I was most evenings, by my little cat family, incidentally the best, most stalwart, and non-judgmental companions I could have asked for. Just beyond the corner TV unit, something caught my eye. Lo, it was a freaking possum, about eight or ten inches long, calmly creeping down the hall toward my bedroom.

My first thought was that it was a rat, so you understand that my second thought was, "Thank goodness, a possum." This wasn't the worst scenario.

The cats, it must be said, did absolutely nothing. I was happy about this for the possum's sake but also a little baffled. I think one of them even gave him a chin lift in greeting. But this was true in the yard too, whenever they encountered one another. Total indifference.

The possum, we'll call him Andre, sees me and scuttles a retreat in the opposite direction from the bedroom, but in my frozen shock, I failed to see where he went exactly. And that was fine with me, because that's when my mind just noped out and made up a complete fiction about That Closet with the Water Heater in It and How There Must Be Some Sort of Hole in There. I was able to convince myself that the possum not only entered my home through a previously unknown mode of ingress no other creature had ever discovered or used, but that he must also have gone out the same way.

I'd like to stress that there is no way a person fully present in reality could believe this — it's far more likely I just left the screen door open too long past dusk. But it relieved me of any need to look for, discover, and remove the marsupial from my home, which was fine with me.

You never know what your limit is. You kind of just hope it's not this, not today. I'd done a lot in the previous four years, so much handling of crises. So much work. But Mark and I had been in it together, you know? I had Another. I was surprised after he died to note how much lower my threshold was on my own. Never mind that everything I know about Mark tells me he'd have been no help here.

But so convinced was I about how Andre entered (and exited) the house, I began to shove towels in the gap under that closet door. I then, and I shit you not, *went to bed*. Yes. I went to sleep with a possum in my house.

She wasn't in her right mind.

I'm not a great sleeper when I'm by myself, and back then I was still in caregiver mode, where the slightest tap brought me fully awake in seconds. With four cats coming and going, I did regular headcounts and doled out head scritches, and the diabetic Louise meowed me up at 2:30am for a feeding, after which I checked if my possum prevention towels were still secure. They were.

There was a cat scratching post at the window in my bedroom, with a platform on top, that all the cats used from time to time. And at about 4am or so, I glanced over and saw the unmistakable silhouette of Andre, looking for a way out. A scant three feet from my actual head.

There was no choice but for me to do something, but after a failed plan to scooch him into a box, and another failed plan to entice him with some cat food, I was at a loss. I thought about scaring him into doing that playing dead thing, but that seemed undignified for me not to mention unfair to him. Finally, with his little back to me, I knew I had to make my move. After a quick pep-talk, I grabbed his tail and lifted.

Immediately, the tail wrapped around my finger, just like it's supposed to, like you read about. It was the coolest thing ever. His head came up, all four feet splayed, mouth slightly open. I walked to the back door, opened it, and set him down. He was frozen for about two seconds, then gave what I swear was a shrug, and walked off, without so much as a backward glance. Success. No one had to die.

I washed my hands and went back to bed.

That Which Doesn't Kill You

THAT WHICH DOESN'T KILL you makes you stronger, you might say. You'd be wrong.

I am not a fan of platitudes in general, for exactly this reason: they are usually something said to a person going through a difficult time to avoid getting into their pain. Platitudes are for generic encouragement, if you don't know someone well, or when you don't know what to say. It could be your own experience makes you ill-equipped to really dig in. But it does handily put a stop to a real, messy, conversation about what is, to be fair, probably something terrible no one wants to face.

That's the purpose of these, I understand. And not everyone who uses them is trying to get out of a difficult talk. We often dearly want platitudes to be true, because we know bad things are coming for all of us, and we hope those things will somehow make us better or more resilient. I'm not going to say they won't. But they *probably* won't.

To be clear, I'm talking about really hard things, the things that come close to killing you but don't. I'm not talking about running a 10K or going through law school. Those are difficult things you elected to do, and even attempting to do them will absolutely make you stronger, but you were never in any real danger.

I think a lot about this quote from André Malraux: "You have not come back from hell with empty hands."

That's probably a little overdramatic for my story, but it's a good line.

I am so risk averse as to be virtually inert. I realize this doesn't paint a picture of a particularly tough customer. And likely that's what gives people the impression that I can't handle the hard stuff. That I'm tender, that harsh language will hurt my ears — can you believe that shit? — and that I should sit down before they tell me The News.

They're not entirely wrong, I do bruise like a peach. But I'm also capable of doing difficult things. I have been tested on that, after all. I've administered IV medications and injections, and I've cleaned up urine, shit, pus, vomit, and blood, barehanded. None of it was particularly easy, but it was just what needed doing. I was there when Mark died, and the only thing worse that I can imagine is to have not been there. But it took a piece out of me.

That which doesn't kill you, as a friend once said, is probably emotionally and financially devastating. Now we're getting somewhere.

There's no such thing as a controlled burn here. Handling this stuff, showing up, soldiering on, whatever you call it — it costs something. It changes people, and not always for the good. It reveals strength you didn't know you had, certainly, and that's something you should absolutely recognize. But it also depletes your reserves, and some are harder to replenish than others. Regardless, I'd wager most people are altered in ways that can't necessarily be fixed. I'm not even sure if I'd want to be fixed. I've always worn my scars proudly; they are literally all I got from this. And I'd be deeply distrustful of a person who'd been through a traumatic event and came out of it just fine.

I think I dealt with all of it relatively well, but I'll never be the person I was before. The emerging me is bound to be burdened in different ways and I have to take care of myself however I'm able to. And there are two sides to that coin. Am I weak because I don't want to be at risk anymore? Or am I strong because I've drawn hard lines around what I will and won't do? I guess it's always about spin.

All survivors bear some mark of what they've been through, even if some people do seem to roll through crises with no discernible effect. Some have good public faces, some — ahem, me — share practically everything with anyone and everyone. But I'll wager that most deal with some kind of repercussion. This stuff oozes into your relationships and onto people who care about you.

I can flip from a roaring confidence to a cowering fear in a single moment. And then back again. I remember complaining about something relatively minor within a year after Mark died, and a friend said, "But Jenny, what can't you do?" I appreciated the sentiment, but the answer would have surprised him. Everything. I was *done*.

Life, it must be said, doesn't really care if you're done or not. It will keep throwing things in your path. (Speaking of platitudes, time heals some wounds but not all, and not all the time, and sometimes it takes, like, a decade or more to even slightly heal from the worst stuff. Who has that kind of time?) But yes, fine, with time I will allow that I feel slightly better able to handle things — when there is no choice.

Oh, great. Another fucking growth opportunity.

The only thing I really wanted and hoped for during Mark's illness was to be there when he died. And I got that — I managed to have his mom, brother, and sister there, too. All of us were by his side. And I held onto that for a long time; I clung to the fact that he wasn't alone and that I got the one thing I wanted. Until I fell apart. It took me more than two years to acknowledge that it was also the worst fifteen minutes/hundred years of my life.

I tell myself that I've already done the hardest thing I'll have to do, but life doesn't work that way, at all. What if I haven't even come close? Human beings live with a certain amount of necessary denial. We all know what *could* happen, but we build a protective mental moat that my therapist referred to as a denial barrier.

She also said that I lacked a sufficient one, and that was probably always true. I've never felt completely safe, but I'm not wrong. None of us really are. My husband had cancer — do you know what the odds are that I'll get cancer? The same as they were before. I haven't earned my way out of anything. It just seems to me that the bad stuff is going to find you. If I seem weird or timid or idiosyncratic, maybe I'm just bracing myself. And maybe it's no one's business but mine.

It's okay. If we get anything at all from having to deal with difficult events and losses, it's the ability to protect ourselves from further hurt. That's cowardly to some, or it could be those people have been very, very lucky so far. They are the same people who tell you about how much stronger you are now. They're off by one letter. It's stranger. That which doesn't kill you makes you stranger.

Weeds

A WEED, I'M TOLD, is anything that grows where you don't want it. In that light, my entire plot of land is covered in weeds.

The backyard is a spacious expanse that everyone seeing it for the first time remarks on with phrases like, "So much potential!" because it really does look like crap. The house has two bedrooms, an office, one and a half baths, a two-car detached garage, and a big yard. Mark and I knew the former tenant through mutual friends, which is how we scored this low-rent LA dream. Many people were interested in taking the place over when the former tenant moved out, but we won, as he explained, because we had both dogs and cancer.

The rent was extremely low. The landlord assured us he wouldn't raise it as long as we lived there, a remarkable gift in this market. The rate wasn't anywhere near what our friends paid for much smaller apartments elsewhere. We felt lucky, and we were.

We did, however, get what we paid for. The whole property is overgrown with fruit trees, camellias, cypresses, and a giant stand of oleander that obscures the entire front of the house. It seems that none of the former inhabitants of this house ever sat down to plot things out or think of the future at all. It's an approach I am perhaps carrying on, seeing as how I too live for right now, maybe next year, depending on pilot season, and earthquakes, and dying dreams. No one ever thought about what it would take to maintain the trees, or what to do when they started dying.

The largest tree is shedding its leaves, so the sun can finally get through. With a little rain, I will soon have some green stuff growing on the ground — I can't call it grass, it's just a carpet of weeds — but it will look so much nicer than the sandy brown soil I live with for the spring and summer. The rain will also bring a few branches down from the old trees. Alarmingly, a big one fell right on the hammock where I like to relax from time to time. On another tree, I can reach up and just pull the branches off. It's mostly dead. I imagine it's still standing out of sheer spite.

An electrical line runs from the house through the back yard, and for a long time, branches swung precariously close to it. On windy nights elaborate scenarios run through my mind about being plunged into darkness, electrocuted, or forced to flee a fire. At least the latter would have the benefit of clearing the land.

After I'd voiced my concerns about this to my landlord enough times, he decided to do the work himself. This is what he always does and also why I seldom call him. He's led by frugality and a mild curiosity about household repair work, but he has no real interest in doing things thoroughly or well. I could take you on a tour of things in the house that just wouldn't be that way if only he'd measured twice. Or if he'd come back the next day like he said he would. This is the man who said he'd paint the exterior when we moved in and then did it *eleven years later*. There's a giant hole in my bathroom wall from plumbing work that was completed over eight years ago. So I only call on my landlord when I really need to, and I'm usually both disappointed and enraged.

In the case of the overgrown branches, he took a chainsaw up a ladder and a branch he managed to cut knocked him to the ground. At least that's what the EMTs and I were able to piece together, since when he came to, he had no memory of what had happened. His wife was furious. He hadn't wanted me to call 9-1-1 so I called her first. "That son of a bitch."

He makes me angry, too, and I think it's because I recognize myself in him. Someone who is also predisposed to take the easiest route, no matter what, and to let things happen rather than make them happen.

After Mark passed away, and I was living alone for the first time in about twenty years, I asked about installing a security screen door in the back. His response was, "They'll just get in the windows." And he was right, anyone could get in those windows.

He shows up every eight to ten months to check in, which usually means puttering around the property without telling me he's there and then scaring me to death.

Years after the tree-trimming incident, he happened to come by on a day when a team of real, professional tree trimmers were working down the street. To my surprise, he contracted with them to handle the backyard overgrowth. I was thrilled. They showed up the next morning with the proper tools and everything. I went out to greet them and learned that only one tree had been ordered trimmed. One.

There's that other one, just raining branches. And the mimosa is clearly on its way to interfering with the electrical wire. But no, "I'll take care of those," he told the man, "little by little." In the thirty years he's rented this property, I'd bet good money that this was the only tree he had trimmed, in a yard full of hazards to life and property.

The landlord listened better when my husband was doing the talking. It took me a while to figure it out, but he's one of those guys. I can see him kind of drift away as I'm talking. When a pipe burst in the front of the house, spewing water like a geyser, he insisted that he never got any of my five messages, and then he was miffed I didn't have the work done by his regular plumber. When I told him the hot water heater was making a loud rumbling noise that shook that whole side of the house, he replied that it shouldn't be because it was only a couple of years old, and that was the end of that. A pat on the head. *You must be mistaken, little lady. You're perfectly safe.* When the heater gave up completely a few months later, he remarked how odd it was that there'd been no warning.

Gosh, it feels good to write all this down. Also, it will serve as some explanation when the house blows up or I'm murdered in my sleep.

Did I mention how he throws any fallen palm fronds from the neighbors' tree back into their yard? I begged him to stop doing that, and he couldn't understand. "It's their tree," he said.

To which I replied, "They're my neighbors." I have to live here, maybe even depend on them one day.

"It's their responsibility," he said, without a trace of irony.

My house is the neighborhood eyesore. And I'm stuck watching the ineffectual bumbling of the man who is supposed to be taking care of it, and by extension, me. He pushes all my buttons.

I don't have the money to fill in the gap on that cheap rent and just pay for the extra stuff myself, or move away, for that matter. After more than a decade, I am like those trees, in one place for entirely too long, with too little attention to nourishment and almost no planning for the future.

There are good lessons in here, I suppose: Don't let the wrong things grow. Not everything deserves your effort and attention. Sometimes a weed is just a weed. Roots are overrated.

Bit Part: Scrolling Along

I AM EXPERIENCING SOME pain in my right arm — middle finger to wrist and along the forearm. For a while there was a surface skin sensitivity also, on the pinky and down along that side of the hand, reminiscent of the peripheral neuropathy that followed my first bout of shingles. It has everything to do with the useless time I waste endlessly scrolling while slumped over on the couch. It's the most obvious ailment, possibly ever, and it's also too humiliating to see a doctor about. I know what this is.

That pinky thing? That's where the phone rests while I check messages or play games. The wrist issue is from the angle of the laptop as I scroll. I am deteriorating while wasting time. Wasting time is hurting me.

I'm jolted by this because I need that arm. I'm right-handed. I'm a writer. It's necessary to all the work I have barely begun doing, don't you see? A major tool of my trade is worn out and I haven't even started really using it yet. And it's not exactly like I hit my thumb with a hammer while building shelters for the homeless.

I want to call it a wake-up call, but it's too early to tell if I'll just roll over and go back to sleep. Still, I have moved the computer into the damn office, where it belongs. I've added a real keyboard, which I'm typing on right now, one of those curvy ones that makes it hard to cling to bad habits. I will shortly be ordering a vertical mouse. I have limited my smartphone staring significantly and stopped propping it on my pinky altogether. All of this will make my time-wasting potentially less physically detrimental. We will have to wait and see whether I'm moved to take that single step from 0 to 1 and just start on one of the major projects I still say I'm going to do.

Sometimes I think I'm just waiting for a cancer diagnosis of my own. I've always worked better with deadlines.

Special Delivery

I HAVE MANAGED, AGAINST the odds, to amass a small nest egg. I have some debt, left over from last year's wild hair/furniture buy that was almost immediately met with a tax assessment and a wildly expensive (and terminal) veterinary diagnosis of the older of the old dogs. And because of that, I'm holding back on my impulse to buy many things.

Periodically, after months and months of judicious frugality, this happens. I'm trying to figure out how to pay down that old debt while still managing to afford a new vacuum, and I'm watching the refrigerator carefully as it approaches its nineteenth birthday. Mostly, I wanted to buy an exercise machine, because I refuse to exercise in proximity to other people. But then the cat stopped eating and literally all the above went out the window. The cycle is a familiar one — get on top by a little bit, go under by a lot.

I have spent significant time unemployed, so I know enough to not complain. But I mostly tread water and it's clear I need to make more money. This brings up a lot of feelings, but the main one is abject panic about finding a new job. It's worth examining since it's obviously blocking my path.

I had been hanging all my employment hopes on a job opportunity, a specific one that met all my needs, one that would save me. For the better part of a year, this job prospect figured into all my imaginings about the life I want. Mind you, it didn't come close to the life I really wanted or dreamed of, but it's what is left. This job is what dreams look like thirty years after you sailed right past that fork in the road. Whatever you do, don't compare the before and after dreams.

I need to come to terms with being a regular person, one with regular hopes and aspirations. A person who mainly just goes to work and comes home and watches television or reads a book. I'm conscious of how many people in the world would trade everything they have to have even half of what I take for granted. But — and I swear I don't know where this came from — I really did think I would be special. Wait, scratch that. I think I thought that I would finally know I was special if I was chosen somehow for greatness. Isn't that how it works? The appearance of a fairy godmother. A visit by a mysterious stranger to the foretold fighter of evildoers. Something that might deliver me, that would validate that little sputtering flame. *You're special, of course you are.*

So, that's it. I was wrong. I'm just like everyone else. And it's not a bad thing, I know that. But I'm so far from what I imagined for myself; I can't even see back to where I lost the way.

Where this job was concerned, I had no power in the scenario and was counting almost entirely on a friend to advocate for me. It took a full year for my hope to waver. I am nothing if not constant, but I finally, finally had to let it go.

Ultimately, I have a terrible fear of the unknown. It's something I can sometimes overcome, thanks to GPS and advance research. But there is a set of things I just can't deal with, and this is one of them.

The risk is terrifying. I don't have a net, but I know intellectually that there's nothing that says I'll fall. Except for my screwy brain chemistry, which is always set at maximum threat level. I am frozen in fear at any new threshold.

I am, I think, even more fucked up than I give myself credit for. I am obviously pretty hard on myself, but I have serious mental hurdles to clear on a good day. Anyone who confided in me about this precise complex network of choking anxieties would get a much more compassionate response than I can apparently manage for myself.

But I pass for normal. So advanced are my coping skills, I even fool myself. From time to time, I catch an aerial view of my life and I can't help but wonder –- why on earth am I stuck in this rut, alone, struggling, you name it. There are reasons but I'm still stuck.

I'm just aware enough to know I'm probably doomed. I need outside help and I'm no good asking for it. On top of all this, nothing interests me. It's not a small problem. Any set of job responsibilities fills me with despair. It's all so...mundane. I can't believe this is all I get. Can't they tell I deserve more?

Snotty, spoiled brat, obviously, yes. But special? No.

The Skinned Knee

THINGS WERE SWIMMING ALONG so well for a while I wondered whether I'd ever feel like writing again. I often go without writing for longer periods, provided there's nothing to yell about. I used to bristle at that old adage, the one about having to suffer to be a writer. But it's a moot point. We're all going to suffer if we live long enough. All of us will get knocked down by something, every single last one of us. Being sad, mad, or hurt has historically worked for me, in terms of expressing myself.

I always think about the kid who is running and playing, and then trips and goes down hard. It's such a long way she falls, going from sheer delight to terrible, stinging pain. And it's not just the physical pain, it's also the injustice, the randomness. Something tripped you that you didn't see coming. And you were having such a good time.

If you're someone like me, you tend to think, "That was too hard a fall. I'd better not run so fast, climb quite so high." No one ever got a skinned knee while sitting on the couch. And I know it's not a good plan. It's not that fun, for one thing, but also, grief and pain come in all different shapes and delivery systems. They will find you on the couch. It happens all the time.

Today is Mark's birthday. I was sailing toward it with a good attitude, I thought. Things have been going so well and in so many ways. But then there was the phone call, the news. A catastrophic diagnosis for someone very close to me. And it's easy to think that I got too happy there for a minute. It feels like the dark stuff lies in wait.

Life is relentless. There's just so much pain in the world, so much of it preventable. It's so hard to turn that off. And the hits keep coming. It's exhausting. If you're not grieving, you will be soon. At least some of those slow gazelles are relieved, they must be.

That skinned knee. It's impossible not to feel just a little bit punished for having fun, for being hopeful. And if you are like me, you have to fight the pull of the couch. The urge to lock it all down, find a way to be safe. I'm just a kid again, the one whose favorite "game" was to be alone in a corner, back to the wall, and left alone.

The Stuff of Life

THIS ALL LIKELY BEGAN in the womb, but for the purposes of this story, I'll say it was first grade. I arrived at school one day and was delighted to find that a thick paper ruler had been attached to the upper section of each of our desks. It was about a foot long and bore distinct marks, a simple sort of learning tool you could easily imagine in a first grade classroom. From that day on, I could hold up a piece of paper or a pen, or anything, and measure its length.

The appearance of the ruler was a lovely surprise. Something we all received, just for showing up, unattached to arbitrary skill sets. It was so *equitable.* Even at that age I knew how rare it was for no one to have to lose.

Being pathologically well-behaved, I was almost afraid to touch the gift, but the same wasn't true for many of my schoolmates, who in no time had added their names and doodles, had punched holes, and drew squiggles, as kids do. It was some time before I felt brave enough to claim mine, and even then, all I did was slide my hand underneath it when I was reading, or during heads-down, or whenever I had a hand free to do so. Because it was mine.

Some weeks later, we arrived one morning to find that many of the rulers that had been vandalized had been removed, *including mine.* Obviously, our teacher had had it up to here with us, the ungrateful children who had not sufficiently appreciated the gift she'd given us. As punishment, we ruler-defilers were tasked with cleaning our desks of the ink and whatnot. There was no ink on my desk, just the telltale gum from the tape, the only sign that my ruler had ever existed at all. I needed to ask for the teacher's help to remove it, which in retrospect is particularly galling. It's like asking your attacker to help you get the bloodstains out of the rug.

Now, the winners in this little drama were the ones who were least impressed with the gift. Those that got to keep their rulers didn't have to clean their desks, so they were rewarded, essentially, for never claiming their rulers as their own in the first place. Dullards. I loved mine, and I lost it. Because I touched it.

This is just one of the contributing factors in my very layered, complicated relationship with Things, particularly the Things I've been given by Others. Our teacher's message was not, "I am giving you this thing. It's yours now." It was, "I'm entrusting this thing into your care, and you will keep it in mint condition until your death." The problem is, I was already wired for that sort of attitude, and the experience with the rulers sealed my fate. I'm convinced it is why I never burn the candles that have been given to me as gifts, such that I periodically have to give away a small stash of acquired candles, and not because I don't like them. It's because I like them too much.

I have this ceramic egg with a blue-and-white design, about the size of an egg. We three Noa Girls each got one in our stockings one Christmas, back in the late seventies. We were tchotchke-oriented and happy enough to have another thing to call our own. I think I need to make it clear that the egg was not in any way a particularly favorite possession of mine. But I've seen to its care ever since. You have to be able to cycle your knickknacks, I guess? Give some away, acquire new ones ... I can't seem to do that.

I don't necessarily want the egg, but I'm stymied as to what else I should do with it. Do people just throw this stuff away? It should be obvious by now that I am not one of those people. If I donated it to a thrift store, would it sit alone on a shelf forever? Who would buy it? No one, which makes me *literally feel bad for the egg.* But there must be someone out there, right? How do I find that person? These questions arise every time I uncover the egg, and in every case, it seems easiest to just put it back in That Drawer. Which is what I have done.

Both of my sisters are pretty sure they still have their eggs somewhere.

If we want to dig a little deeper — and I invariably do — this tendency to hold onto things was reinforced by my mother's habit of cleaning our rooms for us when they got too messy and she was fed up. And by clean, I mean she took a garbage bag and indiscriminately threw away some of our belongings. A lot of stuff I liked went into the garbage. And for a while, at least, I had no recourse, no voice to argue. It's impossible for me, even as an adult, to ask anyone to help me go through my things, or even help prepare for a move. In some way I am still standing there watching my mother throw my things away. Mortified by my choices, embarrassed by the mess.

When Mark very occasionally cleaned out a drawer or something, I carefully picked through the garbage to see what of my things he saw fit to throw away. I was not always rational. Of particular concern were the childhood things — the games, toys, gifts, the detritus of childhood, really. My things are a chronicle of what's happened to me, they hold the memories. And my mother consigned a lot of that to the trash, including my childhood teddy bear. I couldn't save him, and I am not saying it ruined me, but it ruined something.

Studies have been done in which a subject is given a thing and then is offered the chance to trade that thing for an objectively better thing. Most choose to keep the first crappy thing. That's me. Backed by science.

When traveling recently I saw this young family. The mom held the kid's hand, and the dad held the kid's helium balloon. And he was being really cute about it, smiling at the kid, marching along with the balloon. Being a good dad except for the part where he was just holding the string in his *hand*. I was like, "Are you going to tie that string to your wrist, or do I have to do it for you?" Mister, balloons are famous for doing what you're taunting it to do right now. Lose that balloon and you are going to ruin that kid.

My husband was not, despite his occasional wild hairs, much different from me in the collecting department, though naturally the stuff he acquired and kept differed from mine. We were together for twenty years, and in that time we gathered and moved our crap together across the country, all the way from New Jersey, like a glacier. And now he's gone, so his stuff has been imbued with this weighty importance. "I belonged to a dead person," it says, "and he sure loved you." From the Civil War books to the concert ticket stubs, to his grandfather's baseball encyclopedia, I want to do right by everything. That's all I've ever wanted. I'm the

curator of his collection, his history. It sometimes seems
like a huge burden, both physical and emotional. That I'm
ill-equipped for this task should be crystal clear.

I think about it all the time: who is going to clear out my stuff
when I die? And how will I posthumously explain the egg?

"Did she leave a will?"

"Nope. Just a lengthy apology."

The house I live in has been a rental for over thirty years, so
it's a bit shabby. I often fantasize about being able to buy it and
how I'd renovate it, but I think this is just because I can't stand
the idea of packing and moving. Buying this money pit would
be worth it to me to avoid that. Lately, I've begun to imagine a
scenario where I'm forced to move because of the termites, or
the pipes, or the wiring, or any of the other perfectly legitimate
health and safety concerns that might condemn the place.
And I think I would just sell everything, and start over again,
somewhere far away, like England. Or maybe I'd drag my stuff
out to the street and post a FREE sign. What I'd lose in potential
yard sale dollars I'd make up for in not having to have a yard
sale. Which is a fair trade, in my opinion.

Buyer, pitying: "How much for the egg?"

Me, panicking: "It's not for sale! It's a floor model!"

It's clear this is about deservability. If I don't believe I should
have received the gift, that I'm worth the expense, then to sell
or trade or give the thing away is to claim it in a way I'm not
comfortable with. These things don't really belong to me; I'm
just their keeper.

And let's not forget the Earth. How much landfill space should Jenny really get? That ruler is still biodegrading. It's too late for the Earth, I very much fear, but it still matters to me that I'm not contributing more than my share. And yet, no matter what — and this was a huge epiphany for me — whether an item sits in a drawer or sits in a landfill, it is still taking up the exact same amount of space. On the bright side, it seems I've hit a crucial tipping point: I don't want to keep the thing as much as I want it to be gone, finally. Better to confront it, move it along to someone who would like it, or just call it garbage and throw it away. And then *stop collecting more stuff.*

Happily, I am not paying these issues forward. I gift the children in my life by remembering the thrill of that ruler, that simple little something for nothing. And I'm pretty clear on this — it's theirs to do with what they will. If the first act is to pull the thing apart, or roll over it with their Big Wheel, I don't care. I encourage it. I don't want them to keep it forever or attach special meaning to it because I gave it to them. It's theirs to make their own. For gift giving, we'll call it my ruler of thumb.

Bit Part: Teddy

A FEW HOURS BEFORE Mark died, I left his family in the room with him and stepped out to talk to Lisa. She started crying. "If I'd known, I would never have ...."

"Never have what? I couldn't make that out."

"I would never have let her throw Teddy away."

Mister Rochester

MISTER ROCHESTER, THE BLACK cat, is not doing well. He's not in pain, but something is definitely going on, and so I'm swimming in that all-too-familiar pool of anxiety and fear. By now, I've done this a lot, and it doesn't get easier. Knowing that the moment is coming — the one that says, unequivocally, that it's time — keeps me in a weird limbo. Part of me wishes that moment would just hurry up.

I'd planned to take him to the vet today, but I chickened out. See, he's mostly himself. This happened with our big chow-mix dog, Stella, years ago, when Mark and I knew she was riddled with cancer but she, of course, didn't have any idea. She was just her regular old happy self, and we wanted her to have as much of her life as possible, as expensive and emotionally draining as that was going to be. Mister is currently asleep in the yard. It's ninety-something degrees out there and he doesn't care, he's such a lizard. He is napping in the yard he chose about nine years ago. And I want him to have that. I want him to have everything he wants. He deserves it.

I'm sort of an expert at this. The before is awful — their confusion, my anxiety, the not knowing if it's time, then knowing it absolutely is. The during is brutal — the semi-public farewell you have to make at the vet's office, the slipping away, their little bodies. But after is the worst. The giant hole in the house. All the love they took with them. So much of my daily loving attention will be gone. Not to mention that face, that swagger, the meow, and so, so much sweetness. Oh, I'll miss him. I miss them all. It feels like they all just died. I don't know how I've managed with all these absences everywhere.

He was broken and bloody when he first appeared, perched on the wall I share with my neighbors in the back of the yard. He was traumatized and totally opposed to any physical interaction, but he maybe thought I wouldn't notice him. At the time, I had two old dogs, two cats inside, a stray cat in the yard, and a husband with cancer, not to mention a full-time job. The black cat had open wounds at his temples, oozing pus. I went outside to try to coax him closer, toss food to him, and despair. It felt like too much.

"What will you name him?" Mark asked.

"It's Mister Rochester. He's broken and afraid to love again, so ...."

"Wait. He gets 'Mister Rochester' and she's *Yard Kitty*?" he said, indignant on her behalf.

Mister was a good healer, and I promised him I wouldn't ask for more than he was willing to give. And he came around. Did he ever. Very slowly, I was able to move closer to him at mealtimes. And one day I took a chance and slowly reached out to pet his head as he ate. He pushed back into my hand like he'd been waiting for just that, and I've never felt more honored or rewarded.

He has been the sweetest little friend, so openly loving, and the most willing of all the cats to sleep hard on my lap, drooling slightly, for hours at a stretch. He'd run to me when I stepped

outside. I was his sun and moon. His Jane. I adore them all, but he
chose me in a way that the others didn't. My Mister. I am humbled
by his trust. I have no idea where he came from or how he ended up
here, but it was in my yard, even with all its chaotic activity, that
he stopped. His faith in me made me a better person. My heart is
breaking.

I know what probably first drew him to our yard was the smell of
the food I left out for Yard Kitty. But I've always taken him seriously.
He didn't have to come here. He didn't have to stay. He might never
have let me pet him or bring him inside. He didn't ever have to be a
part of the colony of feline guardians who kept me company after
Mark died. But he was. Stalwart, that's him. That's all of them.

So I'm on watch. Waiting to see when the symptoms tip the
scales of his quality of life. I'll try to make the right decision at the
right time. To let him go. It's a hard thing they ask of us, but it's no
more than they deserve. He chose me, and this is the last thing I'll
get to do for him. It hurts so much, but it will be my privilege. To be
fair, to do it well. To say goodbye with as much strength as it took
him to say hello.

Stage Three:

Body of Work

More to Love

Hi, my name is Jenny. I have brown eyes and brown curly hair. I'm five feet, five inches tall, and I weigh a hundred and seventy pounds. At least, that's what I say on my actor resume. It's close enough.

I'm not usually a liar. In fact, I'm a pathological truth teller, but marketing is a funny business, and self-promotion is especially difficult when you don't believe in what you're promoting. In my adult life, I've ranged from 132 to almost 200 pounds, but no matter what I weigh, I feel exactly the same.

I've had issues with weight my whole life. My mother had had difficult experiences around this subject as a child, and I think her intentions might have been good. But she was so clumsy in her efforts, so damaging ultimately, that she essentially repeated history. I remember clearly the first time she commented on my food. I was in second or third grade, dunking a strawberry into the sugar bowl. "You should be careful," she said. Her policing of my intake grew as I did, with predictable consequences.

All this was juxtaposed with my older sister's underweight issues. Suddenly, it was the Clean Plate Club for her, but not for me. The mixed messages were hard to navigate.

I spent a lot of my adolescence on one kind of diet or another, and when I was sixteen, I was put on the Cambridge liquid diet, an extreme calorie restriction plan popular in the 80s and reliably linked to actual deaths. It was prescribed by my pediatrician, a terrifying woman who was even more concerned than my mother about my fate, should I continue down this path. When it was determined that these drastic measures were necessary, I was perhaps a junior size 9. I stirred up my breakfast each morning, and then dumped it down the drain and ate Fritos and Diet Coke for lunch.

A nurse at the doctor's office helpfully suggested that I cultivate a revulsion for how other people look when they eat, as that had apparently helped her to cut back.

[Sidenote: WHAT IN THE EVER-LOVING FUCK.]

I'm not the first person to have parsed this out, but your mother should absolutely not be the person to tell you that you aren't good enough the way you are. I ate more than I needed to, partly to piss her off but also to validate the theory she seemed to be floating, that I would be less lovable that way. My extra weight was a test.

But wanting to be found doesn't mean you're not really good at hiding, or that anyone will be able to see you at all. I was extremely self-conscious, which got in the way of things like dating and auditions, because even I didn't like myself very much. And if that's the case, it doesn't matter what business you're in — you won't get the gig.

Looking back, I can see what a sponge I was. I absorbed virtually every message that came at me, from my parents, friends, strangers, people in ads, characters in fictional television shows, and so on. Trying to assimilate all of this into one world view certainly didn't help matters.

It's no surprise that that little girl might think it would be a good idea to stand up on stage and ask strangers what *they* think.

I had a terrible gym teacher in elementary school, a sarcastic, angry man who regularly made fun of my physical efforts. I hope he at least intended something positive — to inspire us to greatness, perhaps — but unfortunately, I don't think he ever gave it a moment's thought. I wasn't naturally athletic or graceful. I was consumed by concerns about how I looked doing anything, and I made myself miserable trying to please him. Out of desperation, I made more fuss of a hereditary knee condition than was strictly necessary and left the world of physical exertion entirely. I was bussed to and from school all the way through to high school, no Phys Ed. It's still incredibly difficult for me to do anything physical where other people can see me. I wait for the walk signal rather than rush once the blinking orange warning starts. If someone suggests taking a hike, I shrivel up inside. (A walk, yes, but a *hike*? Ugh.) And all the Groupons I've bought and wasted ... oh, the Groupons. From yoga classes to pilates to pole dancing, not one voucher redeemed.

One day, a few years ago, I was seized by the foreign yet unmistakable urge to take a walk around my neighborhood. I made a point to listen to that, like I do when I suddenly feel like writing something down or staying out past 8pm. It's so very rare, it felt like a message from beyond. What if I was turning a corner?

I walked, just a short jaunt, to see if it would stick. On the way home, as I crossed the street in front of a small pickup truck waiting at the light, a man leaned out of the passenger window and screamed, "FATASS!" Over and over, at the top of his lungs, and until the light changed. "Fatass! You fucking fatass!"

There are a few ways I might have challenged his manners if not his sentiments, but this guy was clearly not up for a reasonable exchange, and I was so flustered. I ignored him and pretended to fuss with my iPod, like, "La, la, I can't hear you, I've got my buds in." Mind you, the whole neighborhood could hear him. *You* probably heard him.

Anyway, issues intact, I went home, to share the status update and laugh it off, right up until I cried myself to sleep. Because I hate my ass, too, everything about it. In fact, Violent Person in the Pickup, let me also tell you about my beady little mud-brown eyes, or my stubby, sparse eyelashes. How about these giant earlobes? I smile downward, you know, it's awful. My jawline is softening, and I'd need all day to talk about my neck. Fatass? You're not even trying.

"You look great, have you lost weight?" This question is the worst. Because go to hell, but also yes, and it was hard, and I do feel better, goddammit, and since this is the roughly DOZENTH time I've had to do this, I know it won't last and I feel naked and sad and I miss my shell and I want something for all I've had to give up and food is the only reward I recognize. This is never not complicated.

Growing up, my mother didn't take us to do the big "back to school" clothes shopping trip. In fact, once my sisters and I started babysitting, at age twelve or thirteen, she pretty much expected us to buy clothes for ourselves. Which was absurd, because we made two dollars an hour, a few hours a week. Not enough to buy much of anything, even back then. My parents had little money, and no apparent interest in, or awareness of, fashion, and absolutely no clue about the horrors of a high school social system. This helps explain the shock I felt one Christmas, when one of my presents was a V-neck red velour top. It was right on target — they were totally in at the time. My parents could typically only be counted on to get us a fake version of the thing that was very popular a couple of years before, so this was unheard of. I could hear angels singing when I opened the box.

The shirt was in style, and it was red. Like a flag to a bull. It was terrifying. On its inaugural outing, I was sitting quietly in class when the glowing girl in front of me turned around and acknowledged me, probably for the first time.

"I like your top," she said.

I said, "Thanks."

And then, after a pregnant pause, she said, "It's really bright."

I never wore it again. This infuriated my mother, reinforcing all her closely held beliefs about ungrateful children and the evils of consumerism. I can't blame her. I didn't even wear it on the weekends. I had been told, put in my place. To my disordered brain, these messages reinforced what I already knew: these things are Not For You.

I couldn't handle the red velour top. And velour was really in. And I love red! I knew I didn't belong in that club, a feeling strengthened by the clear message from the club president that I did not indeed belong in that club.

I still can't put together a daring outfit and sail out into the fray without a qualm. Something in me balks. I'm not comfortable begging for acceptance. If I need the right clothes and makeup and furniture and car for you to think I'm worthy, you can go screw yourself. The downside to that is never figuring out how to have decent clothes or makeup or furniture or a car, but one thing at a time, please.

"Jenny has such a pretty face." People started saying this in junior high and high school, and let me tell you, it cut deep. Everyone knows what you're really saying. I was a sponge, as I said, and a teen girl, so the opinions of teenage boys held a lot of sway. And so I reached for all the comfort foods. Fuck you all, but mostly me. For the years of my adolescence and early adulthood, I crushed hard on boys I literally didn't know. I picked someone out of a crowd and hoped that he would pick me in turn. It was the perfect way to stay miserable and alone and to prove to myself that they were right. A pretty face could never be enough. Such a shame.

Anyway, the joke's on them, because that was like, thirty-five or so years ago, and let me tell you, that face is *gone*. Even I can see the difference. You're still going to have to find me, losers! Weight loss at my age just means more pronounced sagging and wrinkles. And anyway, it doesn't matter. I'm not going to let anyone love me, it feels way too late.

I love the body positivity movement, even if my nose is still pressed up against the glass. I know you have to love every wrinkle and every curve, every pound. But how you get there is a mystery to me. You gotta mean it, about every inch, in and out. And I can't keep up. It takes time to gain an appreciation for how you look, and by then, you look different, and it has to start all over again.

I'm assuming, obviously.

I was finally, finally diagnosed with a body image disorder a couple of years after Mark died. It was, on some level, a huge relief. An explanation, finally, for what I was feeling. No solution here, of course. But at least a reason why auditioning feels like a circle of hell, why I dress to blend into backgrounds, why my list of my physical attributes I feel neutral about or like is four items long.

And look: I either have a disorder, or I'm right about all this. I'd rather have the disorder.

So, to recap, my cosmic packet includes: my mother's damaging concern, a terrible gym teacher, mean girls, no money, a bone-deep dissatisfaction with the system, an unwillingness to join any club that would have me as a member, and finally, a clinical condition under the obsessive-compulsive umbrella where the patient is excessively preoccupied by real or imagined defects. It's why some people get so much plastic surgery that they are unrecognizable to their own families. I don't have a clear view of myself; if it is realistic, it's certainly not kind. And it's why I can feel attractive in an outfit before I leave the house but feel like shit once I get to work. It's why many of the items in the clothing giveaway bag still have tags on them. I care too much about what you think because I depend on it to know what I look like. If it sounds exhausting, it very much is.

I find some sympathy for the plastic surgery set, surprisingly. I've always wondered how one could step so bravely into the complete unknown. How could you give up the nose you've known all your life for some nose you've never met? Well, given what's happening with my neck, I'm beginning to understand. Because I wish it were anything, anything but this.

For twenty years I didn't have to do it all alone. I had a husband who thought I was the most beautiful woman in any room, and he told me so, which was enormously helpful. But then he died, and I've had to sail forth without him to anchor me. I mean, it's always been up to me, but it's harder now to do it in a vacuum. It's why I look for validation out there, why I want to be on stage, why strangers screaming from pickups sound exactly like the voice in my head.

Standing outside the magical bubbles of fitness, fashion, and mental health, you'd think I might find some small relief as I age. The jury on my youthful attractiveness and fashion sense may be officially excused. I can't compete anyway, I don't know how, and I never knew the rules. Only that they were inscrutable, constantly changing, and closely guarded by a cadre of scary high school girls.

I've always been more comfortable in hiding. I hide my real weight, my fat rolls, my age. If I have to go out, I wear makeup, I suck in my belly, but eventually, the jig is up. I have to get naked, sometimes for real. And I'm going to get old, if I'm lucky. It would be nice to love all the things I am, it's gotta be the secret to this whole thing, but I haven't figured it out.

I'm slightly alarmed by my knee-jerk tendency, when I see a pretty young woman these days, to think things like, "It won't last," and "Enjoy it while you can," in tones that are not charitable (the voice in my head sounds like an elderly chain-smoker from Brooklyn). But I'm doing okay. I didn't win that battle, but I did survive it. And it explains so very, very much about the last twenty-five years, I can feel relieved even as I shake my fist at the heavens. I just have to try every day to embrace whatever the hell it is I look like. Be okay with what is not strictly beautiful, and try to remember that there's more of me to love than that.

Bit Part: Pursuit

MY MOTHER DIED WHEN she was 47, and I approached my own 47th birthday with a mixture of relief and trepidation. It had been a cloud on my personal horizon for 25 years. It was made more difficult, perhaps, because *she* was difficult. But I also feel connected to her as an artist, or at least as someone who wanted desperately to follow her down that path. We are more alike than I'd have liked, artists of different types who at the age of 47 ended up with a lot of work hidden away. Hers because she couldn't find acceptance for it out in the world, and mine because I won't even seek it. And as I say, the Age It Happened sits in front of you. No matter how you try to turn away, or look past it, it'll float back to the center, like the needle on a compass.

Blue Mood

I WAS A DEPRESSED kid, and I was often labeled as such by the adults. Which is weird, I'll grant you, but thankfully, my mom and dad's path-of-least-resistance parenting style was a benefit in this case. If they were more concerned, I'd have been medicated, and this would be a different rant entirely. Antidepressants have come a long way, but I shudder to think what they were using in the 70s. Cocaine, I think.

We're taught from a very early age to stop crying as soon as possible. It's better (especially for men) to never start. Mothers shush their babies, peer pressure kicks in at school, society frowns, and we never get to cry all the way to the end. I don't think any of us knows how to do anything but try to stop crying if by some terrible circumstance we happen to have started. And I wonder if that's not a part of why so many of us are so blue. I've noticed it runs counter to what I know to be true, which is that it feels really good to cry.

I was a sad kid but not a crier. I was born frightened; my first words were probably, "Is this okay?" I stood back and watched. Then I guessed at some major stuff and got almost everything wrong.

By the second end-of-term evaluation for my grad school acting program, my instructors had identified my Terrible Flaw: I couldn't cry on stage. Nary a drop. They made me cry plenty after classes and at home, but I became convinced that it defined me — as a failed dramatic actress, for one — but also as an unfeeling person. And the more they pushed, the more I retreated. Let me stress, this was not Yale or Julliard. I mean, most of my instructors did nothing to create a safe space or deserve my true feelings, but those types can still mess you up. My mother died the first summer I was in the program. I remember standing next to her body and wondering whether her death might help me satisfy them, and I guess I still haven't forgiven them for that.

When it comes to crying, I think I'm catching up. It may be a little strange for people who took the more typical route. I'm like Frankenstein's monster, coming to life. *Ahh, pain. Fire.* I'm clumsy, and wide open, and it's so scary from my point of view, I can't imagine how disconcerting it must be to watch. But it's new to me, this feeling business.

I can hardly write anything down without mentioning my late husband or my widowhood, and I'd hoped to avoid it here. But. I'm still dealing with it, so you're going to have to, and I suppose I want to stress the fact that I'm not talking out of my ass. I'm not bragging or trying to out-sad anyone — there's quite enough grief to go around — but I don't want you to think I don't have some credentials here. And anyway, this is about floodgates, after a lifetime of plugging leaks. I cried exactly four times during my husband's illness, an average of once per year.

There were a lot of suggestions during that time about things I might do for myself; I was a typical caregiver in that I neglected my own physical and mental health while taking care of Mark. But it felt too risky. I truly believed that it was my tension that was holding me together. I couldn't risk tinkering. There would be time later to deal with it. And it appears that time has come.

It makes people uncomfortable, I think. I suppose a lot of people have thought about how they'd deal with the death of their spouse, and my way probably doesn't look all that efficient. And some may have opinions about how I might do it better, but I'm standing firm.

Because I'm crying it out. I don't want anyone to take this away from me, at least not yet. This is going to sound so pathetic — but honestly, I'm learning what's left when you take away my sadness, depression, and anxiety. Maybe I wear my scars too proudly, but I'm not wallowing or wasting time. I pull it all apart, drain every drop from the lessons, and then I write about all of it. I think that's why I'm here on Earth, and if that's so, then I want to feel it all, good and bad. No shushing.

The last thing I want, on top of everything, is to feel like I'm grieving wrong. Feeling bad about the way I feel sad seems an unnecessary kick in the teeth. We never say, "Why am I so sad?" We say, "What is wrong with me? Why can't I be happy?" Because it's been so long since anyone, without judgment, just rubbed our backs and said, "Let it out."

I am a firm believer in figuring my shit out, but I hope it doesn't sound like I know how *you* should do it. I don't. It's called *self*-help; we're all on our own. But for me, letting go of the idea that I should be done being sad has put me that much closer to being done. The sad is finally taking up the room it needs, and isn't bleeding all over everything else, and I can say that I can't remember feeling better overall. Not for a really long time.

If you want platitudes, I can tell you there's a crap-ton of them offered to the new widow, but this one made sense to me: grief doesn't get smaller. You're wasting your time if you think it will shrink. The trick is to make the vessel larger. Live a bigger life. That is certainly easier said than done, but it feels right. Banishing sadness is a losing proposition. I could devote my life to that climb and never get anywhere. But sadness doesn't preclude joy. Past a certain age, coexistence is probably the best we can hope for. I'm trying instead to make peace, find balance, create joy where I can.

I don't know why I was such a sad kid. But I know exactly why I'm a sad adult. I feel like I'm guarding a shopping cart of what everyone assumes is garbage. But it's not garbage to me; it's not exactly treasure, but it is valuable. Being sad is not all I am, but it's an important part. I'm not asking for more hard knocks; I wouldn't have chosen any of it. But I want to feel things. I want to talk about big stuff, and to cry if I want to, all the way until I'm done. Maybe the best way to be on this ridiculous journey is to take care of the person on it, and to try to respect and love who she is.

The Quiet One

I ALWAYS WANT ANSWERS. I mine for that nugget of gold, the reason I am the way I am. I don't know why it's so important to me, but I'm always going to want to peel back the layers till I get to a center that makes some kind of sense.

My struggle with body image is a tough one. It's a mental disorder, so there's a very good chance it's just brain chemistry. But I hate that answer. I want to believe that with knowledge there's a possibility of a cure.

I weighed just over nine pounds at birth and slept through the night from the start. My dad loved to tell the story about me in the hospital, how I looked like a sleeping purple giant among all the squalling pink infants. My older sister had suffered from colic as a baby, so my ability to down an entire bottle and go to sleep was a pleasant change. Lisa recently said that she feels like she had a leg up in terms of being, ahem, more well-adjusted than I am, because the colic meant she was held more. That is … quite a statement. As I've said, it was a different time. It's kind of a miracle any of us survived the parenting of the 70s.

What a relief I must have been to my parents. I was quiet, I slept through the night. I didn't make demands, I didn't kick up a fuss.

But *of course* I still needed. Of course I did. I was a baby. But my parents were so relieved that I didn't have emergent needs that required constant rocking and holding and soothing, they just left me to it.

I can't know any of this for sure. I'm not saying no one ever hugged me. I have body issues that have dogged me my entire life, there's no reason to think I wasn't born this way. But I can't help but think that things might be better now if that little body had had more actual human contact. That something might have mitigated this cellular conviction that no one could possibly want to touch me.

It's self-perpetuating. Before long, I was expected to be easy, to be amenable, to be quiet. When I needed something, I just put it away. There's still almost nothing I *need*. Nothing I really fight for. I want the minimum, just what's due. But I don't expect it and I won't ask.

Mittelschmerz

IT IS DONE. MY fiftieth birthday is behind me, as is most of my life. I'm not being morbid, that's just math. There is less time in front of me than behind. It can be argued that almost 30 years of that time was just spent growing up. It's the last 20 I have so much trouble with. I can't say I love aging, but it's mostly about having wasted so much time.

Ah, birthdays. They really can go either way. I think of myself as a late bloomer, but more than half my life is over, and I don't feel like I've begun yet. I'm officially quite late to bloom.

So, I'm on the other side of the Big One. Now what? I keep hoping there will be a lightning-bolt moment that will make the pursuit of my tiny dreams okay with me. Surely now? The ticking of that clock seems so much faster.

So far, nothing.

I've read about a u-curve when it comes to happiness, which swings up as one ages past fifty. When, I presume, time and circumstance help us shed the expectations of our youth and we really start living in the moment. It can't get here soon enough. But, knowing me, I'll say, "That looks scary," and decline the ride.

I've caught myself lately making "someday" statements. "I'd love to spend the summer in England," "Maybe I'll retire to..."

So little of it is even remotely plausible, and I'm reminded that I'm not twenty-eight or even thirty-eight, or brave, or financially solvent. These things I dream about won't happen without time and planning and forward goddamn movement, and it's highly unlikely I'll come close to any of them. Hang onto your dreams, people say, and I want to shake them. Because that's not enough. If it were, we'd all be famous. There'd be no homeless people in Los Angeles. But to tell the truth up there, statue in hand, would destroy the myth. "It's luck," I'd yell over the swelling strains of the orchestra as I'm dragged off stage. "It's just luck!"

My mother managed to be a prolific and brilliant artist even in her relatively brief life. I have passed the age she was when she died — with much internal angsty fanfare — and haven't managed to do much of anything. Mom was not commercially successful, though, and deeply disappointed about that. So we have something in common at last. Lots of work in drawers.

Anxiety about achieving more than my mother managed might figure into the mix here, but it's pretty thin gruel. Plus, she has been dead for decades. You think I could be released now, from this pointless concern, hm? Please? On her tombstone, we put, "Artist. Wife. Mother." On mine, I'm thinking, "Polite. Self-Deprecating. Fearful."

I was very, very concerned about turning out like my mother in personality and temperament. I wanted to be an artist, though, and at least part of that is because it was one of the few things she respected. But her example as an artist seemed a terrible one to me. She dedicated herself to art to the exclusion of everything that got in the way, including — and maybe especially — her children. Her resentment was so clear.

My father, on the other hand, throughout my adult life, occasionally mentioned a Painting. As in, "Someday I'm going to finally paint this painting. I've had it in my head for thirty years." Thirty years. How on earth do you do that?

Of course, now I know very well how you do that.

Because of my single-minded plan to move away from all the things I thought my mother did wrongly or badly, I ended up perhaps a little too much like my father. Often, I find myself angry with him not only because I recognize traits we share, but because he never once seemed to strain against his limits. He had an acceptance and complacency that baffles and infuriates me, even though I know he probably had it easier as a result. He never did paint that painting. It hurts me to think about what he might have done, but it's not a stretch to say that the painting had too much riding on it in the end. What possible good can come of finally creating something after all that time, only to be disappointed when it isn't particularly good or necessary or helpful?

To my shame, I never even asked him about the details. Its imaginary state frustrated and saddened me, and it would fire me up for a time. *Do not end up like this.* But nothing came of that fire. Or maybe something did. It's not as if I've done nothing. But it feels like that. My goodness, it really does.

I'm stuck in a cycle: I get ready for work, commute, work, commute, make dinner, stay up too late doing nothing, start the whole thing over again. It's the classic story for so many of us, the silent scream. I am not able to give myself full permission to do certain things, or to do nothing at all. If the TV is on, the computer is open on my lap. I do nothing very well, with intention, with the possible exception of the work I do for other people, for moderate pay. Because it's not even as if I've traded my goals for some big paycheck. I should get a part-time job, perhaps, but I balk at the notion. "Then when would I ...." What?

Writing is the only way I can stave off some of these feelings. Anything will do, but a whole essay or blog post will sustain me for most of a week. Alas, my output is terrible. I can procrastinate whole weekends away, just avoiding the thing I know will make myself feel better. Knowing what to do and then doing it ... well, I haven't exactly cracked that code.

I do so love the symbolic reboot. Here we are on the cusp of a new year, the next project. There's even a supermoon/eclipse thing happening tonight. And I'm 50! Let's do this! Can we? Can I do some goddamn thing, and have it matter, please? Can it be good, and good for you, and fun, and funny? Can it challenge and inspire and entertain and still be meaningful and encourage people to be kinder to each other? Can I do that? I guess I thought I already had. But we must turn in circles, mustn't we? Another spin around. Here goes nothing.

Bit Part: Same Old Same Old

I HAVE BEEN FORCED to Make Changes thanks to the specter of diabetes, and it appears that these changes are bearing fruit. I'm happy with the return on this investment even if part of me is still screaming into a pillow over what I will never ever be able to simply enjoy again. I basically just made a list of all the foods I love most and that is coincidentally also the list of things I can't have any more.

It occurs to me that the first chapters of life are about a loss of innocence, and these chapters I'm in now are when you have to give up everything that took the edge off that sadness and rage. Enjoy your caffeine and sugar and salt and alcohol, kids.

I bought new tops in a smaller size, and I went shopping in my closet and found several things that fit me again. It feels good, but it also feels familiar. I've been on this road before, many times.

Maybe when I get to the next size, it will be safe to just send those things off to charity, not hoard them for the inevitable someday. Emergency preparedness. I have no stored water and one dodgy flashlight, but by god, I have a cocktail dress in every size from 8 to 14.

Hard Eight

MARK DIED IN JULY of 2008. The anniversaries have been hard. Not just because he's gone and I miss him, but because one can't help but take stock. To look back. I can't say I like the view.

So much has remained the same as it was the year he died. I live in the same house we lived in together, with a lot of his stuff, and things we bought or collected together. All of it is getting shabbier. I work at the only job I could get after three years of unemployment following my layoff a few weeks after he died. The job drains me. I can't see my way out of it.

In the beginning, the widow is cautioned to work against the very real urge to make big decisions — selling the house, moving to a new town, sinking all the insurance money in some sort of monument or memorial gesture — but I resisted that urge too well. It seems I've made no decisions at all. It's hard to see what change would look like.

Mark was my change agent. He was my champion. The two of us didn't figure out in time how to be individually successful, but we supported one another. He was a stalwart believer in me and my work. But even with him at my side, it was difficult for me to pursue my dreams, so blocked was I by virtually every neurotic anxiety. Without him? Well, it's even harder.

Part of me wonders if my lack of forward motion has something to do with spite. *You left! I'll show you. Watch while I do nothing.* There's a disconcerting Miss Havisham element to all of this. The comfort I felt at first — in our house, amongst our things — feels more like a haunting the longer I stay.

I can't help but think that all of it would be easier to take if there were someone else who loved me, if anyone had ever even knocked at that door. Granted, I have it pretty well nailed shut. Alone in my self-erected tower-shrine, waiting to be found, insisting that whoever shows an interest must either slay, outwit, or climb something to get to me. Meanwhile, I grow older, less attractive, more lonesome and prickly.

There is another layer in here too — sure, why not? — related to everything I was called upon to do during Mark's illness. The skills I gained from that experience are not transferable, unfortunately — unless I want more of doing and giving everything and not getting anything in return. All that effort and care went into a box on the shelf. It was the hardest thing I'll ever do, and all I got for it is a life alone. And the kicker? No one can tell what I did, what I'm capable of. After all that, I still have to make a case for myself.

Then again, my only patient died.

Yes, this year has been better than last. Yes, I pulled myself out of debt. Yes, I am going on a real vacation. I'm grateful for all of that, and I can pat myself on the back for some of it. But it took tremendous effort. This life is still Not What I Planned. And I'm still royally pissed about it. All of which are good arguments for not marking this day each year. But I'll worry about that next year.

Why/Not

A FRIEND ASKED IF I would read an essay at the end of the month, and I said yes, even though I am trying to stop doing these shows. I'd intended to clear the decks so that I could write something else. I'd love to be able to say I'm too busy, but I'm not doing anything else, and anyway, come on, that's a bit flimsy. You just have to show up and read. Any excuse not to is just that.

The thing is, I'm starting to feel like those shows aren't very good for me. And maybe that's what the essay will be about. A fitting piece for the last performance. But really, why do I do it? I was talking with friends the other night, bemoaning my tiny audiences. One asked why, when I have friends who love me and love my work, I feel the need for a larger audience. And, of course, that's a question for everyone that ever got up on stage. She herself was striving toward creative goals, but I tried not to read too much into the question. What we have isn't enough or we wouldn't be ... well, take your pick: sad, driven, desperate, successful, the list goes on. The creative struggle. If one or two appreciative people were enough for artists, there would be no art at all.

But my question is more specific. Why bare my soul to strangers? Why continue to share more painful and personal information? What exactly am I asking them for? I know I'm looking for connection but I'm not sure it's particularly fun for the audience. Of course they'd turn away from such a naked plea.

Which brings me around to writing something new and different. Perhaps no less personal but a bit less directly linked to my lived experience. And other people can speak the words and I'll be more removed, less exposed.

It feels a little like taking my ball and going home. But I think it might be healthier in the long run. Mind you, I'd have to write something to test my theory. And that pretty much brings us up to date. What's it going to be, and more importantly, when? For the love of Pete, when?

New Year, Old Me

ALMOST HAD A MELTDOWN last night in Costco of all places, not even in the top ten places I would have thought could break me. But it's never about that thing, is it? The last straw is just a straw.

I made it through the holidays okay, even better than I thought I would. I haven't had a big cry in a while, and it might sound strange, but that's concerning. I would like to feel something deeply, I suppose, and nothing is really doing it for me. I was even sort of glad to get sniffly in the car after the Costco fiasco, but it didn't take. In the old days, I'd have blamed the meds but I'm not on anything now.

The theme this Christmas was "be of good cheer if it kills you." I put up the tree and even made a fuss over the old ornaments in a series of social media posts, a trip down memory lane I regretted almost as soon as I started down the path. All that spin about the sometimes bittersweet joys of the freaking journey, when it's really all about diminishing returns. The holidays are never going to stack up to the past, and that's fine, but I'd like to stop having to pretend they do or they will.

I couldn't afford to travel, so I stayed put, and I mostly gifted everyone who gifted me, so that was a relief. I made all the usual resolutions about how I'll do it better next time, and I am sure to fail, which is after all its own Christmas tradition.

Now the new year is yawning before me, and I honestly don't know what to do with it.

The first and only thing on the list is a new job. After that, we can fill in a few more blanks, depending almost entirely on the pay differential. This is an all-consuming prospect, the job search. I need to sell me to strangers, and when I think about it that way, it's no wonder I never change jobs. I wouldn't, as I said, join any club that would have me for a member, and you can see where that would be less than helpful.

I met with an old coworker over the break, and she gave me a good pep talk along with resumé pointers. It was all good advice, but it amounts to embellishing the truth to a degree I'm not comfortable with. I have a low threshold for lying, admittedly, but I am legitimately worried about selling a product that can't deliver as promised. And it all brought home to me that I'm probably dreaming a little too big about the next gig. The idea that I will magically move into a high paying, challenging, rewarding job just because that's where I ought to be by now is ridiculous. It won't matter how many action verbs I pepper into the resume, no matter how many job titles I creatively reframe.

But I need to do *something*. The near total lack of interest in my posted resume is sobering. But the uncertainty, the lack of control, the reliance on total strangers to determine my fate ... honestly, I don't know how anyone does this.

These are the times it's clearest how little I really think of myself. I know there's a diagnosis that explains some of it, but I feel like it goes deeper. It's not just body stuff, at least I don't feel like my concerns are purely about the physical meeting of others (although there is plenty there — we can plan on a nice big meltdown if I make it to an interview). There's social anxiety and imposter syndrome; no wonder I do anything to avoid this. Objectively, I know I'm a good employee, a decent risk, a fun person to have in the office. But in the moment, in the room, I can't hold onto any of that. What I want is a trial period. I want to prove myself, not talk about how I might do that if given a chance. Please let me show you. With a little training and some time. I can morph! Helpfulness is my office currency! Wait'll you taste my scones!

This is Going to Hurt

OUR FAMILY DENTIST WAS a great guy. Funny, personable. All five of us, my parents, two sisters and me, visited him every six months. This was my mother's doing. My dad had grown up with free-clinic dental care in New York in the 1940s and, suffice it to say, he'd never gotten over it.

Of the three of us girls, I was the cavity kid. Now, I'm the least likely to make regular dentist visits. Why? Because never, in all those cavities, did our funny, nice dentist give me a shot of Novocain prior to drilling. I didn't even know people did that. I don't know why he didn't, although I now wonder if it wasn't my frugal mom's idea of a cost-cutting measure.

Anyhoo, I have a high threshold for pain.

I had to have some surgery a while ago — pretty routine stuff, nothing to be concerned about — but it was surgery. General anesthetic, abdominal, with all the pain and discomfort that comes with that. I'd been promised a little PCA pump of morphine, and frankly I was looking forward to that part.

I'm a very cautious user of all drugs, prescribed or over the counter. I will endure a headache for hours before it even occurs to me that they have pills for that. It's like the one thing the medical establishment can point to with pride. We can fix minor headaches! But I have deservability issues, so pain relief doesn't always occur to me, and furthermore, I seem more interested in knowing why something hurts than making it stop. Headaches disturb me; what exactly is hurting, and why? It's your head! Migraines sound like hell on earth. How have we come to accept them as normal? You tell the doctor it feels like your ears are bleeding, and the doctor says there's nothing wrong? No wonder people go for the stronger stuff.

With my hang-ups about aspirin and its alternatives, you can see that recreational drug use was out of the question. I've always harbored the conviction that any foray into illicit anything would be literally the death of me. Like if I decided to have, say, a second glass of wine, I would get alcohol poisoning and die. Similarly, with drugs, I think, okay, I'm going to do it. I'll inhale, or let it ... dissolve, or whatever, I don't know the jargon. But that would awaken the undiagnosed aneurysm, and I'd end up in a coma, a cautionary tale. And with my experimenting days roughly thirty-five years behind me, I've missed the chance to really figure it all out. So, when I had to get surgery, I thought some supervised drug-taking in a medical facility was my chance, finally.

Turns out, medical professionals use the word "morphine" interchangeably with "painkiller." Sort of like if someone asks if you need a Kleenex and then gives you a freaking *Puffs* with *lotion*. I ended up on a baseline level of Dilaudid, apparently part of the morphine family but stronger, with an extra pump when I wanted it, but no more than every fifteen minutes.

I am no fan of pain, but pain medication is something I do not tolerate very well at all. I was loopy on it, and shocked when I learned it was Dilaudid. They'd given it to Mark a couple of times during his cancer, and he'd hallucinated — a known side effect. It was infuriating. It seemed like the meanest thing to do to someone who's hurting. Isn't it bad enough they're in the hospital? They're in pain or facing death, and you have to turn them into a clown on top of everything else?

I pushed that button because I felt like crap, but it didn't make me feel better. It just messed me up in a different way.

The nurses asked, "How are you feeling?"

And the answer was, "How the hell should I know?" Only it came out, "Something something koala bears." Frankly, I preferred the pain.

After a few hits, I put that pump as far away from me as I could, and as soon as I could make myself understood, I asked to be taken off all of it. The anti-inflammatory the doctor prescribed did the best job of easing the pain, and I could ask for Vicodin when I wanted. Which I did twice before deciding I couldn't tell the difference.

Surgery *should* hurt. A doctor sliced into me and removed what he called a "humongous" fibroid tumor. "They paid me extra for how big that was," he said. You've heard of the grapefruit-sized tumors? If you need to put a face on those, make it mine.

The day after the surgery, according to protocol, they "pulled the catheter," and just like that it was up to me to get to the bathroom. The nurse was helping me up the first time, and as I swung my legs over the side of the bed, I thought, *Ow, OW. YOW. There are staples in my belly that were just put in yesterday, this effing hurts.* I wondered if I should stop moving. But the nurse was unperturbed, and I am a kiss-ass, and I still had to urinate. And by golly, I went to the bathroom and produced a quantity of pee they were strangely eager to measure. But it was a lesson — things are going to hurt. It's a foregone conclusion. There's no way to avoid it and still live any kind of a life.

Most drugs aren't painkillers. They're just distractions. I'm not advocating for going without them, I'm really not. I have relied on antidepressants before, and I likely will again. If there is something that can help you, and you feel like you need it, then by all means, do that. Take the Novocain. But I'm trying to be careful about erasing my feelings altogether or distracting myself with nonsense.

I don't like to shush crying babies. I mean, I'll feed them and change their diaper and try to figure it out, but if you're just in a mood, I encourage you to feel your feelings, kids. As an adult, you'll be lucky to get the chance to cry most things out, let alone get to do it at full volume while being rocked and adored by someone who'd die for you. Seriously, at the end of a very long life, you'll be able to count those times on one hand. So have at it, I say.

A large part of my midsection remains numb from the surgery, and it disturbs me, worse than the swelling or the doctor's use of "humongous." I'm told it will mostly come back, but not all the way, and not to wish for it too hard, since it comes back with pain. Fine, bring it. Turns out I'd rather feel something than nothing.

Bit Part: Circle of Concern

I SPENT A COUPLE of days this week running around, trying to check all the to-do list boxes before the weekend. This mainly consists of going off campus at lunch to do shopping and running errands on the way home, and it makes for an exhausting time. But I had to ask myself why I was doing it. It was clearing the weekend, but for what? Honestly, I don't have an answer, not one I like. I wanted, most of all, not to have to do anything. That's it, my dream. To do nothing. To sit on the couch, read romance novels, and protect myself from any real demands on my time or effort.

It's all well and good to be on a hamster wheel. It's the way of the world, really. But I can't help thinking that in the best cases, the wheel powers something else, something fun or creative or interesting or helpful. And me, I'd rather do nothing.

I have joked before about my Circle of Concern™. How if an injured animal or something stumbled into the Circle, then it was out of my hands, they were inside, mine to take care of. But I feel like that circle has been getting smaller and smaller. I patrol stingier borders. Maybe it's a reflection of the state of the world right now, but it shames me. I imagine re-drawing this map one day. When the home base is sound, when I'm comfortable in my skin.

Down Girl

I RANG IN THE new year with one of the deepest depression dips of the past year or so. There didn't seem to be one regret, loss, or fear I didn't dwell on. It was short-lived, at least, but hoo-boy, it was jam-packed.

And instructive. I spend so much time beating myself up for all the things I have not done, all the failures of time management and decision making, it's so easy to forget how far behind I started. I don't give myself any credit for that, because, ultimately, I don't acknowledge the reality of clinical depression and anxiety. Oh, I accept it in the abstract. I respect it in others. But I have been historically unwilling to give myself the same level of understanding. Mental illnesses are difficult for even the afflicted to accommodate, never mind other people.

I've been reluctant to use them as an excuse, although occasionally they are exactly that (e.g., why I don't want to go to that party, why I can't seem to get off the couch, and so on), and they are always, at the very least, a factor. They are part of my equation, and I should remember that, especially when self-flagellating and making unfavorable comparisons to other, more successful people.

"There's this big reason why you fail," is not exactly a comfort. It's easy to go too far down that road and convince yourself you shouldn't bother trying. But it's time for me to stop searching for the magic something that will fix this. I've spent so much mental energy digging for the source of the block, the reason for my depression and anxiety, thinking that it will be some magical fix. That I will be undammed as a writer, that I will be willing to leap creative hurdles rather than turn back. But that's not going to happen; this is it, the only life and chance I have. It must be a better use of my time and energy to work with the tools I've been given rather than wish for ones I don't have.

I can hear my therapist's voice in my head. *Jenny, can you find a way to be compassionate with yourself?*

So that's my resolution, to try to stop asking why these mood shifts happen and concentrate instead on the more helpful questions: how I can lovingly care for myself when they do, and what I can reasonably expect to do when the fog lifts.

And it *is* lifting, of its own accord. It always, always does.

Full Exposure

I AM WEARING SLEEVELESS shirts this season, a major breakthrough for me. I almost called my therapist just to let her know, I was that proud of myself. This is a big deal because I hate my arms. Bluntly, with the exception of four features I either like (hair, boobs) or am neutral on (nose, feet), I hate nearly everything about my physical form.

I know; I don't need anyone to tell me this is fucked up. I haven't been in a bathing suit in over fifteen years, and even then, it was a jerry-rigged, shorts-and-sports-bra affair, to cover my most egregious faults. No one but my adorable, pool-obsessed, four-year-old niece could have made that happen. I am fully clothed at the beach, it's my thing. I love being in the water, but I hate feeling exposed more.

I can expose my inner self with no problem. At least it's something I'm far more willing to do. I want you to see me in that way. If I can possibly win you over with my thoughts and feelings, then maybe you'll excuse my swells and dimples, wrinkles and scars. I *hate the package I come in. Let's make a deal.*

It's a shame that courage comes with age. Cour*age*. Because now that I'm finally ready to show my arms, they're a lot worse than they used to be. It should not be considered brave to show up somewhere in your own skin, in an outfit you like, feeling pretty or sexy or whatever. But I can't do any of that.

We are told to love ourselves, and I hear it, I do. But it isn't a fix for everyone. How on earth is a person supposed to get there from here? And this isn't even about beauty or desirability. It's about whether or not this body is worthy of love and care. I took intimate care of my husband's ailing body for years before he died. But I can't imagine anyone doing that for me. I can't imagine anyone wanting to.

I have disordered thinking. My image of myself isn't accurate, which means I have to depend even more on other people's opinions. And, well, I'm an aging woman who lives in Los Angeles.

On one hand, this could be freeing. I'm mostly invisible to people around me, and I cultivate that. Full coverage, no patterns, nothing trendy. But when I do on the rare occasion step out in something noticeable, it is a big deal, it feels brave. "I'm here," I say. But no one seems to notice these efforts, which is perhaps a relief but also deflating. If no one mentions my colorful, patterned blouse that I thought I liked and was flattering, my panicked mind can come up with only a few reasons for that. By the end of the day, I'm exhausted. I can't wait to cover myself back up.

As a kid, I latched onto stories where the heroine is revealed, like Cinderella at the ball. She was once invisible, then she is seen, finally, and from there, loved. Coupled with my clinical diagnoses, this is a recipe for disaster. No one's life is a fairy tale, I know, but I expect more from revealing myself than is possible. I'm also a flawed, aging, dimpled thing. Who should care, exactly, especially if I don't?

Brains

OK, I GUESS WE should talk about It. It's a body thing, but really, it's brains.

The disorder itself — body dysmorphic disorder — is characterized by an obsessive concern about real or imagined defects. Sometimes it is about a single feature and sometimes it's several features or more generalized.

I always operate on at least two levels: doing the thing and wondering how I look to others while I do the thing. This usually starts the second I leave my apartment and continues throughout whatever occupies me until I get home again. I am a notorious homebody, but that's because it's necessary to relieve the strain. I need to get home. But it's not a perfect fix.

My current, rather charmless, apartment is like a lot of other moderately priced rentals, in that the landlord opted for the least offensive and least expensive decor. For my dwelling, it means beige textured walls, stucco ceilings, patterned Formica counters in the kitchen and bathroom, and mirrors. Lots of mirrors. Like, there must have been a sale on mirrors, they had to be giving them away. Avoiding them is next to impossible. My comfort level at home is directly linked to whether or not I'm within view of a mirror.

Obsessive reflection checking is a feature of this disorder, and I did that a lot when I was younger. If you don't know, you need to check, right? As adolescents, a friend caught me looking in department store mirrors as we passed them and called me vain. I sputtered. She assumed that I liked what I saw. But I was checking because I did not know what I looked like at all. Now, I avoid mirrors as much as possible. I turn away in the changing rooms. Catching my reflection in a storefront window, say, can be a shock. I've changed entire hairstyles after one glimpse.

Another part of the disorder is believing all the normal human functions are somehow worse on me. For example, the way the hair grows on my legs or armpits is uglier and more objectionable than the average woman. More disgusting. I convince myself that my deodorant is failing, that my body odor is overwhelming, but I don't detect anything once I'm safely at home.

What happens if I have coffee breath, or I sing off-key, or I can't get that sportsball all the way back to you in one throw? Well, nothing, obviously. It doesn't matter, it doesn't reflect on me as a human being, how deserving I am of whatever humans deserve. But in my head, it's the worst thing that could ever happen. It's damning. It confirms some essential truth. It's not that I'm a perfectionist — I think we're all pretty clear on that by now — I'm just crystal clear on what you might not like about me, even when it's all perfectly normal, human stuff. I'll tell you in advance, if I ever disappear into a hermitage, never to be heard from again, it will be because I farted audibly in public.

I don't think I'm a superficial person, but I sort of expect everyone else to be, at least when it comes to me. There are fundamental things wrong with me that I can't expect anyone to overcome.

The more makeup I have on, the worse I feel. But I can't wear *no* makeup either, obviously. Sometimes I do go out with nothing, on the weekends, to run errands or whatever. It doesn't feel great to be out there unarmored, but it's a trade I make to avoid the chore of taking it off. And if it helps me blend into the background, go unnoticed, all the better. I am conflicted: I balk at the idea that I look better with makeup on, but I can't deny it. There's a tipping point, though. If I go too heavy on the eyeliner or brow pencil, foundation or blush, I feel conspicuous and ridiculous. A clown. *Look at her, trying so hard. Who does she think she is?*

I still feel like I'm lying when I put mascara on. *I have really short lashes*, I want to tell people when I meet them for the first time. *None of this is real.* I can't show them my plain, unvarnished face, but I also don't want them to mistake my made-up face for the real one.

I need one of those magnifying mirrors to apply my makeup, and that's hard even for regular brains to process. There's no escaping what's happening on my face as I age. I can't say it's helpful, but I can't see another way. I just can't see well enough, on any level.

Makeup, shapewear, contact lenses, fashion in general — it all seems pointless. We are going to have to take all this stuff off, you know. And I am pathologically honest, but maybe that's the crux of it: which version is the truer one? It shouldn't be controversial that we might like to enhance some features or disguise imperfections. We are, in fact, encouraged — some might say made — to conform.

There's no way for me to know if what I see is what you see. And that makes any kind of confidence I might have in my appearance disappear. My mirror lies. *Maybe.*

I undertake all physical activity entirely in private. I don't take walks through my neighborhood, though I can walk with others with less self-consciousness; I'm not even comfortable rushing across a street. There are people in those cars! What else do they have to do while waiting for the light but to watch that woman crossing in front of them and form an indelible opinion?

Anxiety over new things completely overwhelms my interest in doing new things. I sometimes panic at the last minute before parties at new-to-me locations. Part of this is due to the actual walking in by myself: my body, entering the room, not knowing who is there, what they see. That is the biggest hurdle.

I am not particularly graceful. My gross motor skills — running, jumping, climbing — were never really well-developed. I do have decent body awareness, but of course I do, I'm hyper-aware of my body in space. I also had some movement training as part of my MFA. In the yoga class I took (very) occasionally with a friend, I responded to subtle corrections in ways that surprised the instructor. *Lengthen your spine, your hips should be blah, blah, blah.* All of that was easy for me to translate, because to be out of control of my body is among my bigger fears. Locking it down, remaining contained, that's my starting point.

I am essentially never completely naked, other than in the shower. I'll even pull on my panties before unwrapping the towel. I am careful to shut the door to the shower/toilet area. This is separated from the sink as it would be in a hotel, but it is blissfully mirrorless in this little space. Because I live alone, there's no one to see me but me. No reason to shut that door, except for the mirror in the other room that I can see. That I imagine can see me back.

Skin picking is another symptom of my disorder, and that's where I really shine. I can't let a bump live. I focus mainly on face and neck — which is to say, I deliberately hunt them down — but if I find one anywhere, I'll destroy it. Lately, I've focused on my lips. I'm as horrified as you. Yes, skin picking leaves a much more noticeable wound in place of the bump, but I think I'm okay with that, because at least it communicates that I've seen the thing, the blemish, the imperfection. It's so you know that I know. An unacknowledged bump is laughable. *Poor her, she doesn't know.* It's like spinach in your teeth, but for your face.

Possibly related or maybe a whole separate thing is an irrational concern with my physical safety. I remember sleeping over at a friend's house as a kid and trying to explain that I felt anxious not only because I was facing an uncovered bay window at night, but also because there was a shadowed expanse behind me in the large room. I felt entirely vulnerable to attack. I still remember their expressions. That was an "Oh, this is just me" moment that really stuck.

So I'm uncomfortable in large rooms, particularly if they have big windows. I don't mind an open plan as long as it's a small house. I just prefer cozier spaces. People love those big houses on the beach with floor-to-ceiling windows and all I can think is, *where are the drapes?* I can't be comfortable at night if the windows aren't covered, even if they face the ocean. I see those fancy, expensive houses and I think, *It's a fishbowl. Those people live in a bowl.* I'm sure they'd defend it by saying how relaxing it is by the water, but I'm pretty sure I'd never have a moment's peace.

Video meetings at work are especially hard, and I avoid turning on the camera if I can. I've noticed that my face looks different to me than it does in video calls with my sisters. My eyes look closer together and are angled oddly. It's a miracle I can contribute at all, if I even do.

I have dimpled thighs and varicose veins. My eyes — my *eyes* — are losing pigment around the edges. All of it makes me worse; It's proof of something. I was so very susceptible to the stories I was told as a kid about who is worthy of love and how important their beauty was to that equation.

I have an abiding love of romance novels. For me, reading about people loving each other in spite of their flaws is deeply, deeply therapeutic. I am always reading at least one, but more often, there are several going at once. They counteract the internal voice. They're medicine.

You know how you see a photo of yourself, and you think, "Ugh, is that how I look?" I feel that, multiplied by a thousand. I was once caught unaware on a birthday video someone took for my boss and it made me cry. I gave away the sweater I was wearing in it. I reset the gauge every time that happens.

I always wear very plain clothes. Nothing flashy, almost no patterns, nothing that could be mistaken for a stab at what's fashionable. Sensible shoes, no heels. No tottering around, clip-clopping, no drawing attention. It's so much more special when someone finds you, I'm assuming.

That's a tiny joke. You may be wondering how I managed to find a boyfriend/husband. Here it is: dint of will. I was late to the dating party, and he was someone I'd known for a long time and felt I could trust. He understood what was difficult for me, and he loved me to pieces. He also thought I was beautiful, and that didn't hurt. But any interest other people showed up to then (and there were very few) was met with panic and retreat. I am now so heavily defended no one could get in even if they wanted to. But no one wants to, they don't even think of it. The dating pool is extremely small in my current age range, but I don't think it would matter, not even if I lived in Alaska. My walls are sturdy and tall.

Being seen or observed without my knowledge is a horror. I realized recently that this transfers to my home. The idea of people there when I am not — apartment maintenance, the house sitter — is completely unsettling, sometimes to the point of tears. Them seeing my stuff, me not there to defend or explain — it's like being naked in front of them. I mean, I guess. See above, I'm almost never naked.

I sing only when I'm alone or in company whose love I don't doubt. Same with dancing.

You can have this body image disorder with any body type. I am now a size 12, around the average size for women in the US, but I have always felt like a giant, the most conspicuous physical presence. I entered college, after a very focused summer, at 132 pounds and left grad school at 150 or so. I have lost weight and gained it back countless times. Ninety-five percent of people who lose weight gain at least all of it back, plus a little extra as punishment for thinking you could ever belong to that club.

Globally, the beauty industry is worth upwards of $400 billion. Hair care, cosmetics, fragrances. We are practically required to hate ourselves; entire economies depend on it. So you keep trying, investing. "Be your best self," they say, but the odds are stacked against you. The clearest messages suggest that your lovability and fuckability depend on your weight. There is a part of my brain that has bought into this entirely.

I think I'm at my set point. Side by side with my sisters, I don't eat much more than they do, but I outweigh them by probably 40 pounds. My habits are good ones in general — we have diabetes in the family, and my blood sugar levels flirt with the red zone, so my diet is about oats and nuts and beans and greens, plenty of high-quality proteins, and little in the way of starchy sugars. But none of it works the way I've been promised it should. I had a bracing chat with my doctor about body acceptance and just living my life and staying active, but she still wrote "Patient is obese," in the notes. The BMI chart still hangs on the wall of her exam room.

You'd think that improving my body would be a priority for me, but it is so fraught. I want to be strong and flexible, but to do all that requires intimate work with this thing I don't like and feel so separate from. It's a battle to do anything at all.

Did you know that research primates — with strictly controlled and consistent diets — are bigger now overall than they used to be? There are factors at work we can't control, don't even understand. I do understand this: cultural notions about weight and beauty are designed to fuck with an obsessive mind.

All this is for sure a boner killer, but in the wrong hands, it's also a weapon. You can see how dangerous it would be to hand myself over to a stranger.

When the Covid-19 pandemic hit, I felt like I'd been training for quarantine my whole life. Masks were a welcome accessory, especially as I couldn't help but murder the mask-ne bumps that appeared as a result of them. High stress makes the skin-picking worse. Lockdown was a reprieve. I left my face alone. I convinced myself I was losing weight — I wasn't, but isn't that fascinating? Absent witnesses, I could accept myself.

Whatever beauty I had is fading, and aging brings with it so much more to disdain and feel self-conscious about. I was hopeful that there would be a lessening as I got older, an abatement in the constant noise. Freedom. But no, it's only gotten worse.

Mind and body exist separately for me. In a perfect world, I'd just be a brain in a jar. The reason I stand up on stage and tell total strangers my deepest secrets is the same reason I overshared with those high school acquaintances. I want to make a case for myself separate from what you can see; to sell you on what's inside in the hope of making up for the outside.

I'm trying to earn the space I take up, the food I consume. But who loves nakedness, really? As you get older, your truths, inside and out, get harder for anyone to take. So many scars and marks. And I know those make up a map, I know it's better to have lived and that it's okay for it to show. But I don't like what it looks like on me, and I don't expect you to either.

What if I make you laugh? Wouldn't that count as *useful* if nothing else?

The only time it's quiet is when I'm on stage. It's no wonder I chose acting, but it's also no wonder I was doomed from the start. I don't know why my dreams survived my total inability to pursue them, I really don't. I guess it's a kind of self-medicating, isn't it? I could imagine a world where none of this interfered. Where I'd won, somehow. Where I'd have proof of my worth. There was no choice but to stick it out.

But presenting my physical self for someone's approval is the thing I cannot do. Like, if we were to boil down my disorder, that's the sludge that will stick to the bottom of the pan. And the fact that I'm aware of it is not particularly helpful. It's like being trapped in a cave and having just enough light to see how impossible any hope of escape really is.

I can't say, in any context, "What do you think about this?" I mean, I want people to love it, cast it, fuck it, but I can't ask for any of that. Because I despise every inch of this. The best thing I can say for this body is that it houses a decent inner person, but even that belief will falter, and I have been necessarily (to my mind) protecting that person. You see how there's no real way out? It's a tower too high for anyone to climb. What I do instead, I suppose, is write paragraphs like this one.

Bit Part: Just Look at Her

I AM BEING MOVED from my office at work to sit in an open bullpen with the others who, like me, occupy the lowest rung on the workplace ladder. I predicted this, based on some new hire activity, but that doesn't lessen the ignominy of shuffling armfuls of your belongings down the way. Down, down.

I am trying to be patient on the job search, I am. I know that just because I'm ready for something doesn't mean the path will reveal itself. But goodness, just for freaking once it would be nice if things happened as I wanted them to.

I am a victim of circumstances, actual and pathological. And there is a niggling feeling that I should move. Somewhere cheaper, that's easy. But somewhere no one knows me.

Anyone who knows the bare bones circumstances of my life knows that something –- maybe lots of things -– went wrong. I think I could fake it if there was just one element that spoke to normalcy. A house of my own. A romantic partnership. A decent job, a hobby or interest I actively pursued. But I don't have any of those things. I'm a middle-aged administrative assistant with no apparent ambition or drive, no sustainable interest in anything outside my cave. It's obvious.

So the dream is to show up somewhere new, with a new, portable job. And fake it. But can I really move to an unfamiliar city where I know no one? I've done it several times before but never alone. Even then, I could never tell if I was running to something or running away. But does it matter? Maybe it'll be an adventure. Maybe no one will think I'm in witness protection or that I'm a hopeless, stagnating, would-be something, who is missing that One Thing, whatever the fuck it is, that magic ingredient. But I don't think so. They'd be able to tell something went wrong for me in life, those new neighbors and coworkers. Anyone could, just by looking.

Figueroa St 1 Mile

WITHIN A WEEK OF starting a job at the college where I'd end up working for eight years, I was introduced to a potential carpool pal by another new coworker. I could not imagine a worse fate, and not only because I was being manipulated by strangers.

I was just rejoining society after three years of unemployment, which followed four years of caring for Mark while he had cancer. I'd failed totally at pursuing my own creative dreams, even when I had the time and space to do just that. I'd sunken into extreme debt and mental exhaustion. I had to sell a car for rent money. I was finally hired at my lowest personal point. The job didn't pay enough, but I was drowning, and it was a lifeline. I was both deeply grateful and wildly unhappy. I needed time. Specifically, at the beginning and ending of each workday.

My new coworkers were baffled by my frozen horror at this rideshare prospect. There was a real cash benefit provided by the college that we'd both enjoy, and it would have been a way to go easy on the earth. But, but ... my alone time. My songs. How on earth could I be compatible with someone who saw no downside to losing that time? And just where would I make it up? In my *cubicle?*

Yes, I lived alone. Yes, I spent most of my free time by myself. Not the point! Car time is different.

One might think the best thing about cars is the adventure and freedom they represent. But for me it's really about the cozy nature of that space, a feeling of safety — illusory, I know — that was probably forged when I was floating in daydreams in the back seat of my father's car, watching the play of shadows as we passed under the streetlights on our way home from Grandma's.

As a kid whose favorite game was to sit quietly in a corner, it's rather obvious. I'm somewhat in charge in the car. It's a controllable space, and it provides cocooned alone time, thinking time, music time. Those elements can be had at home, of course, but the flavor is different. I drive safely, of course, but I can be on autopilot much of the time. Even though I'm handling a large and lethal machine, there is a lack of distraction I don't find in many other places.

I am not a small-talk person. I am never going to be happy talking about nothing with a person I hardly know and don't necessarily want to get to know better. How could I be asked to do that for *an hour a day*? The very idea of carpooling is an introvert's nightmare, but there was more to it. At that moment in my life, my commute was especially important to me, because that was when I did most of my crying.

The person I was being paired with was not remotely a good fit for me. When we realized during the usual new coworker chit-chat that we lived in relative proximity, she immediately said, "We're going to carpool," in a tone that suggested the conversation was over. This was a mistake on her part. I don't react well to that kind of presumption. She explained that the school would pay us each

$50 per month as long as we shared the ride at least ten times. I applaud this, in principle.

This was not the only time I shot myself in the foot, fiscally speaking. My financial difficulties during my underemployment period could have been handily managed if only I'd gotten a roommate. But I couldn't. *I couldn't.* I'll take poverty for no reason, Alex. I need to poop in peace.

As I floundered through a discussion about routes, I suggested that the one I took might be shorter than hers, and she said, quote, "When it's your turn to drive, you can do as you like."

I know it's not her fault that she reminded me of my mother. But it's not mine either.

It's not my job to make myself uncomfortable so that others can have what they want. This is a lesson I often have to relearn, because it's my nature to see to others first. And when certain people don't get what they want, they'll make me uncomfortable anyway. That's the loop.

What I wanted didn't seem to matter, but at this point, I'd been *through* it. I couldn't give even one more thing away. I went home feeling pressured and angry, and boy, oh boy, did I use the hell out of my car crying time. Could I — and I seriously thought this — simply pay her $50 a month to leave me alone?

To the confusion and consternation of these brand-new coworkers, I somehow managed to mumble excuses and avoid the subject until they finally got the message. I was proud of myself in the end, and I still am. It's not easy to stick up for yourself, though admittedly, it gets a little easier as you get older. You can pretend it's just idiosyncrasy, make excuses or don't. "No" is a complete sentence. People won't always understand. Sometimes even you won't.

I suspect I'm not the only one who does this, but at any rate, I recommend choosing a spot on your commute when you'll know it's time to pull yourself together. You can wipe your eyes and get your head in the game, so no one at work will suspect how you've been using your car time. Mine was Figueroa St 1 Mile.

Appeasement

THERE'S A PERSON AT work who doesn't like me. We did get off on the wrong foot, and I think I know how, but reasons only work on the reasonable, and he is not that. He made up his mind and there was no going back. I honestly don't like him either, but a) he started it, and 2) I'm a freaking ray of sunshine. I'm not blowing smoke when I say I'm universally beloved at work.

Setting aside that he's a poor judge of my character, he is also a known liar, temperamental, and borderline creepy to a few of the younger women on the team. And yet, here he stays.

It's bringing up a lot of stuff for me.

In every workplace, it seems, as in every family, there is at least one person that saps everyone else's energy, morale, and happiness. Life can become, to a certain extent, about how we navigate these individuals' tender feelings and the threat they pose to the general welfare. Sometimes it's the CEO of the company, or the president of the country you live in. Sometimes it's your mom.

I admit to being something of an armchair therapist, and I believe my coworker has some undiagnosed shit of his own going on. But most of these Problem People have personality issues contributing to the situation. That doesn't make it easier to live with. It doesn't put you in less danger.

The thing that eats at me is that he lied about me to our boss. He was cornered and became defensive, and he lied. I'd already reported the incident so ... it didn't impact me at all. But it didn't impact him either. And that's the trap. Most of us are so polite we can't call out liars with even half the confidence and bravado with which they lie.

Appeasing this person is safer than challenging him, and no one gets that like I do. I'm a born appeaser. I can't list all the ways in which my sisters and I made ourselves smaller so my mother could be as big as she wanted to be. And that's at least partly why this is wearing on me. I can only watch as his responsibilities increase, his work is praised, and he's handed the keys to the castle I've been toiling in for seven years.

This happens all the time, everywhere. Angry people end up winning because the community is motivated to keep them from getting angrier, or in extreme cases, violent. There is a tacit understanding among the group. *This person is unsafe. We must adjust.*

This is my wheelhouse, by the way. Ask me anything. With an angry, depressive mom, it was almost impossible to predict how she'd blow and what small transgression might cause it. So I appeased, and I lost the ability not only to voice an opinion but even to identify what that opinion might be.

Perhaps the worst thing that came out of this was that all my efforts worked. I became the favored child, and as a result I think that all I am worth is what I proffered for my safety. If I am quiet, nice, helpful, and funny, I can win some level of affection (read: security). It has worked, for the most part, but the natural consequence is a bone-deep doubt that that regard is real. I am left wondering what I'm really worth — all my parts boil down to currency. And, of course, when literally anything else is required, I'm at a loss.

None of my usual tricks work on my office mate, which is fine. That ship sailed, and I have no wish to curry the favor of mercurial weirdos, thank you very much. But I'm struck by how little all my hard work matters when it comes to how other coworkers treat this angry person. I have their good favor, but it doesn't feel like much of a win when I watch them bend over backward to try to make this guy feel special and happy. But I've done the same thing, been in their shoes. I get it. There are few choices when one is under threat.

Maybe people like him tell themselves that they are looking out for their own interests, that they deserve this consideration, for whatever (possibly good) reasons of their own. But they never acknowledge the fact that they've allowed no room for anyone else to do the same.

Growing up, we all scrambled to keep my mom on low simmer. It was a survival thing, I can appreciate that. But it did some damage. There's a cost to the appeaser; the whole community suffers. And the irrational person never seems to know a transaction has taken place. They only register the loss of their unchecked freedom to be or do whatever they want. None of this is new, but I am seeing it a bit more clearly lately. Maybe we all are.

I know a lot of this is about workplace hierarchies and systems of labor. No one wants the discomfort — the work — of firing my coworker, or the hassle and expense of hiring and training someone new. In these situations, people like him get away with behaving exactly as they please and end up carving their own experience outside all the norms and customs of the group. Everyone loses except for the irrational one, who is often given things like more responsibility and attention — essentially rewarded for bad behavior. I'm the best-behaved person you'll find, and I can tell you the rewards over here are few. But I'm amazed and fascinated by the extent people will go to so someone else doesn't get angry, all the ways some of us contort ourselves, sell our souls, even, for just a little peace.

Bit Part: Guilt Trip

MY SISTER WAS USING accumulated credit card reward points to plan a visit to LA, but she felt guilty about taking the trip. And I gave her the pep talk, but I knew exactly what she meant. Who are we to take these pleasures?

Do I deserve success and happiness? Why not? Who the hell is keeping score on that? No one. Plenty of people deserve more than they will ever have, and many others have way more than they could possibly deserve.

Jeff Bezos thinks he's a decent human being and I worry about whether I should order the appetizer. Whether my simple pleasures are some sort of affront.

Elena denying herself a trip doesn't make anyone else more able to do anything. Me writing all of this down may not serve anyone, but that's not a good reason for not writing it down. Where does it come from, this inability to see ourselves as worthy of the absolute minimum?

One of my mother's favorite admonitions was, "What makes you think you're so special?" Maybe it's as simple as that.

Evaluation

IT'S EMPLOYEE EVALUATION SEASON. I'm supposed to fill out a form about my work and career goals. It's a tall order, and historically nothing is worse for my morale than having to answer these questions, which are stated as if this job was a choice I'm satisfied with and that I'm a regular person who is looking for advancement. I'm not. It's all I can do not to write *THIS WASN'T MY PLAN* in red marker across the page. Instead, I have to write down my career goals at this job I didn't want in the first place and that I now don't know how to leave. Some days, I feel like I'm good at it. I'm built to make sure the way is clear for other people to be successful.

And yes, that means I share in that success. But it also means I don't get paid very much, and the recognition smacks of ... well, it doesn't feel like real recognition, does it? "I couldn't have done it without Jenny," is often code for, "I don't know how to clear a paper jam."

It's endlessly fascinating to me how the foundation of almost every commercial venture is a group of people getting paid the least. The corporate world runs on administrative support. But what am I really worth to them? Sadly, I use their measures, as I always have. I'm worth what they tell me I'm worth.

My willingness to accept that is what makes me an ideal employee. Never a squeaky wheel. Plod along, head down. And predictably, I don't have a lot to show for it. I don't think anyone is indispensable, but I really strive to be needed. The easiest way to get there is to be the office catch-all for the stuff that no one else wants to do. They call me Jenny Noa'r of All Things. It's affectionate, and I like it; I want to be needed, I do. But I've also made myself into the drip pan of office grunt work so that I can feel secure, and I'm not remotely secure. Like most people, I'm a single paycheck away from total financial disaster. They don't even have merit-based salary increases where I work. The longer anyone works there, the worse their life gets. I wrote that into the self-evaluation one year. It's math, but it's cosmically perfect for me. Even if I could dredge up the nerve to ask for a raise, the answer is a policy-based "no." It's the all-too-familiar one-way street of caregiving, wanting what's just not possible.

When I'm in a bad mood, I think I'm just like a person who can tie shoelaces. It's an important job, a necessary one, but it's ultimately something everyone can do. Mine stay tied, it's true. I have a special technique, a patented loop-around tie that just doesn't come undone all that often. But my coworkers don't know that. They don't have to. They're too busy running ahead.

Needless to say, looking for another job feels like an insurmountable task. To look at a job posting, decide I'm right for it, apply with confidence, self-promote. It's like it's designed with me failing in mind. And then I think, let the resumé speak for itself, right? Post it online and let them find me ... among the roughly three billion resumés. It's comical, if you like dark comedies.

It happens that there have been some recent changes in the office and a lot of the admin stuff is being scraped off my plate. My boss — who's a really decent guy, that was just luck — is working on getting me a title change, which is the only way to get more money. Which you'd think would be fine, except I'm in a panic, because I'll be asked to hone skills I have no experience with and because the tiny raise won't materially change my circumstances. But I can see myself staying here even longer, just because someone finally checked in on me and realized I needed something. What won't I do just to know how that feels?

Nobody Cares

WHEN I WAS SET free from grad school, I was also set adrift. I had no concrete plan for what would happen next, a failure of imagination, perhaps. I'd assumed, as was (is) my wont, that the next thing would come from all the hard work I just did. The path would reveal itself. Someone would see the show, cast me, offer ... something.

I was in a very small theater market. I think there were perhaps five professional theaters when I graduated, and despite a good reputation in general and good reviews for my work, it was hard for me to muscle my way in. This should have been a sign, but I couldn't read it.

The summer after I graduated, I was dismayed by the jobs on offer in the summer festival the school produced. I should explain that this was not unusual. We were lured to the institution with the implied promise of hands-on education performing each summer, but in reality, we were little more than set movers. The festival aspired to greatness, and I think it sometimes even got close enough, but the yearly snubbing was a source of some bemusement.

We train actors we wouldn't hire!

I declined their offer of a job and spent the summer instead nannying for the daughter of two out-of-town actors who'd been cast in meatier roles. (Hoisted something something petard.) It was brutal. I'm okay with kids, but not precisely gifted, and we had trouble finding a groove. She wasn't easy, and I was in a tailspin. Plagued with stomach pain, a stress response to the last months of school, I had no idea what would happen after the summer.

I ended up waiting tables, which made me reminisce fondly about the babysitting. I was forced as a server to check the IDs of students I'd taught in my Intro to Theater class the semester before. I brought them their pitchers of beer. It pained me to be such a cliché. And I was panicked and miserable, because I didn't know how to move forward.

As I was dragging myself through my shift one day, my boss called me into his office to tell me in no uncertain terms that everyone could tell I was unhappy but nobody cared. It was the best piece of advice anyone has ever given me.

He didn't mean there was no one *on earth* who cared, only that no one *at work* did. Not him, and certainly not the customers, who sought a convenient meal and the bottomless soda refills and the Cajun shrimp n' pasta, but did not come to be waited on by a slouching depressive. Essentially, he was telling me, know your audience.

I'm amazed to this day that as sensitive as I am to personal criticism, I didn't, even for five minutes, hold that little chat against him. Indeed, I felt better immediately. It's possible I just wanted one person to notice. But also, it really was good advice, and it has served me well. People didn't come to that restaurant to get a complete understanding of all the ways I'd been let down. Strangers don't really care why you're sad or late or tired.

Here's the really hard part: even your closest friends don't always care when or why you're upset. You may strain their patience when you try to confide in them, particularly when you circle the same subjects again and again. Nobody, even if they love you, will care about the same things as you forever, especially not the things they see as solvable with their perfectly functioning brains. I'm still mortified about the number of times I complained about the same things, with no clear idea how to fix them, or that they were up to me, or that they were tedious, worn-out subjects everyone was tired of. I still feel bad about that.

I ended up paying a licensed professional to listen, which I can't recommend highly enough, if you can afford it and find the right person. And I wrote a lot of things down in a semi-secret blog I now heartily wish I'd never told anyone about, but it still worked out pretty well, as a lot of it ended up here in this book. In any case, these are my recommendations. Put on your workplace smiley face, collect your tips or paycheck, and remember that nobody cares. You'll thank me one day.

Stage Four:

Corpses of Hollywood

Please, And Take it With You

As WITH SO MANY childhood stories, I'm still learning from *The Wizard of Oz*. The older I get, the more deeply I seem to feel Dorothy's struggles. Maybe I can blame it all on "Somewhere Over the Rainbow," one of the simplest, most beautiful songs I know, and performed flawlessly by the very young Judy Garland. I was a kid who was arguably too impressionable for the message. *Birds fly over the rainbow. Why, then, oh why can't I?* It's that "Oh, why" that really gets me.

An ordinary girl wants more and sets out to get it. Despite meeting some wonderful characters, she gets sort of broken by the experience and ends up returning to what is familiar and secure. Hm.

Interestingly, but maybe only to English majors, Dorothy's path from the farm to the big city and back again is, in literary terms, typically the boy's rite of passage. If I remember correctly, the girl's story most often ends in marriage. I did get married in my story. Mark and I set out on the road together, but he died about fourteen years in, after almost four years of illness and struggle. I've never worked harder in my life than when I took care of him, but the reward (if you can call it that when your only patient dies), was just that: the knowledge that I'd done a difficult thing. Similarly,

I've always been extremely well-behaved, and to my surprise I've learned that all you get for that is a shining record of good behavior. Not quite what you hope for, but there it is. Sometimes the thing itself is the only prize.

Mark died in July of 2008. I was laid off from my job two weeks later, and just like that, I had nothing to do. There was no one but me to take care of, and a little pile of life insurance money to stave off panic and finance my journey. And I thought, *well, here you go. Time to figure things out, and maybe carve out a living doing that thing you said you would do.* I'd dreamed of being an actor for as long as I could remember, and while I spent many years dabbling, and fitting it in where I could, I was finally free to concentrate all my efforts on making a living doing this thing.

It didn't work out quite the way I planned, I'm deeply sorry to report. I'm not as intrepid as Dorothy, it turns out, and the path was not nearly as clearly marked. Though I was creatively busier than I'd ever been with improv, writing, and auditions, the money dwindled. I began to panic, and before long, I was looking for paying work. As an underemployed freelance copywriter, I spent the better part of a year cursing my ill-timed lapse in employment and beating myself up over my apparent inability to chase my own dream.

Job interviews are very like auditions, lots of guesswork and acting the part — and often the idea of winning is more compelling than the role itself. But I finally found work in the fundraising office of a local arts college. I may be one of those people who can't be happy anywhere, but I was clear-sighted enough to be grateful for almost everything about it. Good people, a sense of shared purpose, and artistic endeavor everywhere. But ... a career? My life's work? Well ... it didn't make my heart sing.

It's the performer's life, you know. Day jobs. Just for a bit, only until you get your big break. In one of the many books I read about how to make an artist's life, it said that should you need to work to pay your bills, you can and should strive to do as little as possible at your job. You should do only enough to keep it, and use the extra time to see to your real goals. But I have never been able to manage that. I threw myself in. I am not just eager to please, but fearful of displeasure. I work for anyone to the exclusion of everything else. But it was easier to think that those jobs were what got in the way of my creative work. I was so worried that a job would become my life, and then my dreams, or whatever they were, would be left by the wayside. To compensate, I made sure to never take the promotion —- always stay low, so you aren't as beholden. "This way I can go on auditions," I told myself. That I never went on auditions was a knot I couldn't untie for a long time.

It's possible to stay focused on your dreams while handling the practicalities of life. I know this because I've seen other people do it. But I'm on my own now. There's no savings account, no other financial support. I have dealt with catastrophic illness and just came through three years of underemployment. I need a steady paycheck and health insurance. It's not cool, which is probably why it's taken me so long to come around to it. Not that I'm generally cool, I'm not. I just inexplicably chose to take a stand in this area. The artist's life looks fun.

But this new job didn't sound so terrible. It could be a regular life, a grown-up life, where I buy things with cash and pay my bills on time. And when that niggling little doubt would surface, "What about the stuff that makes you happy?" I reminded myself, I haven't been happy yet, so let's just see what happens, shall we? My thinking was warped by decades of yearning for something I had no idea how to get. The witch's broomstick. I wish it were so simple. Surrender, Jenny. Take the job.

The hardest part is getting used to not yearning. My dreams may have been unrealistic, but they were there. They took up room. I'm not quite sure what to do about the yawning space they left behind, and I catch myself feeling like a total waste of air and food. What was any of that for?

Hollywood. The Emerald City. Where the dreams that you dare to dream really do come true (ahem, for a statistically insignificant number of people). I realize now my dreams were never specific enough. I thought I was special, that I'd just need to show up. But I was ill-equipped for the journey. You need to be able to convince people of your worth. This is not only *not* a strength of mine, it turns out I'm viscerally opposed to doing that. I think you should just love me, and if you don't, then I think you should just go fuck yourself. And that attitude, good people, will only piss off the wizard.

My friends were so encouraging about the job. I mean, it had been a long haul for them, too. They'd been on Widow Watch for a while there. They told me I deserved it, but I don't know what to do with that. On one hand, I'd think, *Do I?* I mean, for this particular job, I waited and relied on a friend on the inside to sell me for me. That's the only reason I got it. But on the other hand, I'd think, *Is this seriously all I get?* I have been so well-behaved! This can't be everything. It just can't. Why, oh why, can't I?

Dorothy Gale should've known from the start of that yellow brick road how things were going to go, and I should have too. Who builds a road made of bricks through a forest? And what is that pointless spiral at the beginning all about? Just start over there, Dorothy! Everyone can tell you're wasting your time. Ugh. Apparently, in life, you just have to go in circles for a while. In front of everyone. (And then through jungles while avoiding flying evil to this magical city where a wizard might grant you a wish, but only after you do the impossible, and by the way, he's lying.)

At the end of the film, when they ask Glinda why she just didn't tell Dorothy the way to get home in the beginning, she says, "She wouldn't have believed me." As a kid, I thought that was such a cop out. We were watching, Glinda, and you didn't even try. For the longest time I thought they were just covering a hole in the plot, that the person who couldn't help her in the beginning could suddenly do it now.

But now I get it. She had to believe that there's no place like home. The magic wouldn't have worked because Dorothy didn't yet know that statement to be true. She had to live a little. And in the end, she had to say goodbye to some things, and if you're like me, you can hardly stand it when she does. "I think I'll miss you most of all," she says to Scarecrow. And the reason that's so sad to me is because even though it's true, it has no bearing on her leaving. Sometimes we have to move on even though it hurts.

There were never any guarantees that I'd get the bright and shiny world I dreamed of. I just wish ... well, that's it. I just wish.

I mean to figure this happiness thing out, and if I'm lucky, it'll be the right-now type of happy and not the *if-only* kind I've been living with for so long. When it gets me down, I try to think about the end of the film, when Dorothy wakes up in her familiar, albeit less-colorful, world. All the things she thought she'd left behind are still there. They look different, rooted as they are in regular old reality, but they are a comfort to her and part of who she is. And that will always be so.

What a world, what a world.

Bit Part: Math

To be a working actor, you need consistent validation from total strangers. That's how it works, and if you want more than that — such as money and fame — then you must grow that audience of approvers exponentially as you go. That's the math. If you're someone whose happiness and self-esteem is also tied to these external forces, then the actor's life will be more difficult for you, not least because you care too much about the opinions of others to be able to do your best work. Not caring is the key to getting the gig, everyone will say so, but how do you set aside how much you want something in order to vie for it? I don't have an answer to that, I'm afraid.

People who say you need to want it enough will also say you have to care less, let go of thinking you can control the outcome. Which answer you get depends entirely on what you're complaining about that day.

Like many actors, I decided on this path at a very young age. I let my four-year-old self steer my ship, and she brought it all with her — the insecurities, the shyness, the wounds. All of that held me back as an actor, but also protected me, which has taken me years to understand. Because the things I was after — to be chosen, to feel loved, to have some control — were not to be found on the path

I'd elected to follow. I was wrong about it, but in my defense, I was four.

There are probably very few successful actors who are happy with what they have. (Stars! They're just like us!) The luckiest and most talented A-listers probably also have a list of grievances. Parts they wish they'd been offered, awards they thought they should have won, unhappiness with the way they are perceived. Dissatisfaction is built in.

You remember what it was like when you were little, when you did something and the grown-ups cheered. It feels *so good* when everyone claps. It feels like a drug that can heal things, one that can close wounds.

Corpses of Hollywood

ESTIMATES VARY, BUT THERE are likely over 200 bodies on Mt. Everest of climbers who died trying. I've been obsessed with these people for years. Given the extreme conditions above a certain elevation, they can't be removed, and so there they stay — along with empty oxygen canisters and actual garbage and feces — on the mountain. A recent effort removed 20,000 pounds of trash, but it barely made a difference.

Climate change has brought even more deadly conditions and melting snow is uncovering more bodies. If you're looking for stark, unspoiled beauty, you'll have better luck on any of the other Himalayan peaks, any of which will be just as happy to kill you.

There is an area on the northeast ridge known as Rainbow Valley, because of all the brightly colored hiking gear on the bodies dotting the area. People must pass them on their way up, and – if they are very lucky – trudge by them again on the way back down. The way down is even more treacherous than the ascent, which makes sense because you're that much more frozen and oxygen deprived. It can take 12 hours to go one mile.

The people who make it back often say things like, "I knew I could do it," and "you can do anything you put your mind to." They trade on it for the rest of their lives. It's on their CVs, they embark on motivational speaking tours, never mentioning how big of a factor luck is, or the team of Sherpas they paid to handle their gear and fix the ropes and sometimes literally carry them there and back. But okay. You did it.

Those 200 dead climbers thought the same thing. "I'm going to summit Everest or die trying," they said.

There's a cave along one route known as Green Boots Cave, because the body that occupies it is wearing green boots. He is believed to have been part of an Indian expedition during May of 1996, the deadliest month in Everest climbing history, a record unbroken until 2014, and then 2015, and then 2023. They're pretty sure they know who it was, but now he's a corpse of Everest. A very well-preserved body they say was heading back down from a successful summit. In any case, I'm sure Green Boots' loved ones are consoled by this wonderful legacy. I mean, you want to leave something that will last forever. Not everyone gets a cave named for them.

And then there is Hannalore Schmatz. In 1979 and at age 39, she was the oldest woman to summit Everest on a German expedition led by her husband. On the descent and separated from the others, she sat down and died just a hundred meters from Base Camp IV. So ... for over twenty years, anyone climbing the southern route would see Hannalore, leaning against her pack, hair whipping in the wind, eyes open. Regular decomposition can't happen at that altitude, but wind and sun exposure take a terrible toll. Don't look it up, is what I'm saying.

An effort was made to remove her body in 1984 and two people *fell to their deaths*. Eventually the wind took her over the side, thank goodness. I imagine it was really casting a pall over the mood at base camp.

"Well, they knew what they were getting into." That's the rote, glib response. Anyone climbing will admit to the risk, but I'm not convinced that they think that deeply about it, if at all. Very few of us have been on the edge of death or have watched someone we care about gasp out their last breath. If they do consider it at all, it's overwhelmed by their certainty that they will make it because they are special. We all want to believe that. There are stories of climbers, stranded and freezing, begging those passing by for help, and those people ... just passing by. "They knew," they think, handily hopping over thorny moral questions. We're just not built to think we aren't going to make it, despite the direst warnings. Despite what all our acting teachers said in almost every class, despite the odds provided by family and friends. What we really think is, not me. I'm special.

Oh, sorry. This essay is called the Corpses of Hollywood. But it's about one in particular.

It's impossible for everyone to make it to the top, there's just not enough room. We've all heard the stories about those who step on others in order to make it, and that might be true nearer to the summit, in what they call the Death Zone. But down at Base Camp One, where I've spent most of my time, we can afford to be each other's champions. We tie ourselves together and pretend we won't cut the line should someone stumble into a crevasse.

It's a big party at Base Camp One, a never-ending stream of show invitations, podcast launches, and film screenings. And it's creative and fun, a nice club to be in. But I can only marvel at these people

– their perseverance and energy and confidence – none of which I possess. That level of effort is necessary, if exhausting, but success is still a ridiculous long shot, and that freezes me in my tracks. Can anyone see you, really? Why even enter the fray? I've been outside all of this from the start, unwilling to impose and therefore a virtual corpse. Is she breathing, alive? Doesn't matter, just keep going. We can't do anything for her now. She knew what she was getting into.

I'm pulling myself out of this climb, but it will be as if I were never here. That's the way it works. Red carpet, summit. Potato, potahto. Can they even see us from there? Do they survey the bodies? I mean, for my little comparison to hold, we're saying those in the top tier, the A-listers, only have a few minutes to enjoy that view and pat themselves on the back, knowing it's likely they'll die on the way down, scratching and clawing, while the latest crop — still with a little strength and some canisters of oxygen — sprint past to the summit.

When I see a homeless person dragging their cart down Fairfax, I can't help but think, what's your screenplay about? What was your dream? I mean, we're all walking through a graveyard. But you could also say those folks stuck it out. You don't fail in Hollywood, the old saying goes, you just stop trying.

I am done trying. I am tired of being invisible. I am tired.

I suppose I like this image of myself as some sort of sacrifice on the climb. Jenny, stuck with old Green Boots. She tried but couldn't do it. There is a reverence among the climbers, real or not, for the fallen. But I didn't fall. Arguably still at the first Base Camp, I never even zipped up my parka. I was given this partial package; some of what I might need, but none of the necessary stuff – hustle, I think they call it – any interest at all in competing with others, or the ability to step out from the crowd and make people look at me.

I spent way too much energy on the Mountain of Self Doubt and forgot all about the March of Time. It has to be okay for someone like me to make the call and get airlifted off this rock. Find a patch of earth and live out my life without having to watch everyone get or not get what I was never going to stake a claim to anyway.

We've all heard the refrain. Some people have it and some don't. It took forever for me to realize we aren't always talking about the same "it." Whatever it is, some are right about having it and some are wrong, but they all believe. Those that are right may still not achieve very much, and a lot of those that are wrong do anyway. It's a crapshoot. Nature doesn't care about you, and neither does Hollywood – there's no option for those that have some of it, but not all, and those folks rarely also have what it takes to recognize it and make changes. That's me. In mountaineering, it's called an on-sight climb. I must figure it out as I go.

If it's true – if you truly believe that if you work hard, you will get what you want, then the opposite must also be true. If you don't have what you want, and you're nowhere near it, then you must not have worked hard enough. And that can do some real and lasting damage.

There isn't enough work for the people who believe their happiness depends on it, but we still beat ourselves up every day over not getting a tiny share. It takes forever to make the call, because it's a seductive argument. We all do have something unique to offer, but that doesn't mean the world won't keep spinning without it. I'm coming to accept that. And here's the surprise: it feels pretty good. There's such a stigma about quitting, no one talks about the crushing weight that lifts when you finally let go of what isn't working.

Now, at bedtime, instead of asking myself, "What did you do for your dreams today, loser," I say, "I'm sleepy." It is a change for the much, much better. The phrase, "death of a dream" sounds way worse than it really is, especially when the dream is all wrong for you.

The most heavily invested of my friends will say "don't give up," but if all I've really managed to do is greet the newcomers and bow them along, then what's to give up? Illusion. I'm getting off this ridiculous mountain, covered in dead bodies and garbage and poop, actual poop. You go on. Bundle up. I will watch your web series, but I'm going to be over there.

There aren't many areas where failing is better than trying something new, but the Hollywood dream is one of them. Because we've convinced ourselves we should want to die trying. That's how you get respect on the mountain.

There was the body of a woman 800 feet below Everest's peak. She died in 1998, the first American woman to summit Everest without the use of supplemental oxygen. Her summit still makes history, even though she died within a day or two on the way down. Her husband also died, probably trying to save her. He was a world-class climber they called the Mountain Lion. It didn't matter. Oblivious first-timers make it back down with nothing worse than a frostbitten pinky. Life isn't fair. Hard work is just that. You should prepare and condition, yes, but it will only get you as far as luck says you can go.

Her body was there on the trail for nine years. It became a landmark if you were climbing the Northeast Ridge –- you know, I'm an hour below Fran, that sort of thing. She became known as Sleeping Beauty, a horrifying reframing that says a lot about what can happen to your soul at the summit.

One of the climbers who'd happened upon her when she was dying went back in '07 just to move her body off the trail. He'd never forgotten her, but how could you, traipsing past her every climb? It was a nice gesture, but I'm not sure she'd thank him for it. She made it, you know. She's famous. Some people will take that any way they can get it.

Bit Part: Everyone's Dream

YEARS AGO, A DEEPLY funny and talented friend of mine told his girlfriend he wanted to pursue a career in entertainment. She was, shall we say, not receptive. When he explained that this was his dream, she said, and I quote, "But that's everyone's dream." It felt shocking at the time, I remember, and the blunt dismissal was naturally something of a blow to him. But I can't help thinking it stuck with me for a reason.

I'm not advocating for diminishing the dreams of your significant others. But I think she was right that everyone has a hopeful something. Everyone wants to be a star. Recognition, applause, whatever it is. Is there anyone who hasn't imagined it?

My friend was deflated. He ended up breaking up with that girlfriend but also abandoning the dream. It had been, I think, still too new to withstand the onslaught. He might have done wonderful things in entertainment, but I'm pretty sure he did wonderful things anyway. We lost touch years ago, but I wonder if he still feels a little pang. I envy him. Better that than this.

Real Talk

THE AUDITION IS A special circle of hell. It begins with the surreality of entering a waiting room full of people who look a lot like you. It's like standing in front of a funhouse mirror, minus the fun. Imagine a nightmare where you're forced to fight the spitting image of yourself for your own future. That's the beginning.

There are often terrible people in the audition room, who don't look you in the eye, who are constantly on their phones, or eating lunch. It's your job to impress people who have a jaded world view or have cultivated one to fit in with their peers.

To get here in the first place, everyone in the waiting room has likely taken a class or a series of classes in commercial auditions. The instructor probably mixed over-the-top encouragement ("You're going to book everything," mine said) with stern lectures. They excel at the tough love schtick, the "real world" hardness, giving students a dose of the prescribed medicine. The instructor tells himself that this is what he's paid to do, that it is, in fact, a kindness. You feed on the crumbs of encouragement peppered throughout the dick behavior, and you fool yourself into thinking you're doing something right. *I've arrived*, you think. *I can do this.*

A reminder that intermittent reinforcement destroys the minds of animals in lab experiments and is a factor in, if not at the heart of, all dysfunctional and obsessive relationships.

I don't think any artists are more willing than actors to pony up hard-earned cash to people who'll be mean to them. We ask for it and eventually are conditioned to trust only negative feedback. That one one-star review holds more sway than all the effusive praise. We didn't necessarily start out as the most insecure people you ever met, but some of us will get there pretty quick.

Whatever your profession, we all walk around with the running list in our heads of ways we haven't quite measured up. For the most part, our parents, teachers and bosses are happy to spell out our flaws for us. And we'll join in. You wouldn't believe the shit I say to myself. Actors are unique in that they are encouraged to gather up these criticisms *on purpose*. It's built in.

There are very clearly people in charge in the audition scenario, and it's not the actors. We had to beg for this chance to humiliate ourselves, and it's hard to make a case that we're not being punished somehow. We're treated like children. Line up, sign in, wait patiently, toe this line. It feels like a test and in many ways, it is.

But the only way out is through, right? *They'll start treating me well once I'm through the door*, we imagine. *They'll refer to me as* the talent. *I'll have arrived.*

Until then, you have to care about how you're perceived by people you don't care about. It's not healthy. If you are, like me, a little too concerned about what others think of you anyway, it's a hard road. How, oh how, can you do your best for them? In two minutes of desperate pantomime?

In a recent commercial audition class, I was exhorted to always be my true self, and was assured that indeed, it was the only way I could ever hope to book anything. I'd accept that but for the fact that they want you to do that in a setup so completely artificial, it feels like a joke.

"OK, you're in a car, except it's a chair, and the wheel is on this mike stand, and it's not really attached so you'll have to hold it between your knees for the taping. There are kids in the backseat you can refer to through the rearview mirror, but there obviously aren't any kids, or a backseat, or a rearview mirror. Don't mime anything, please, but we should see the car. You need to act like you already booked it or that you'll be out of town for the shoot dates — confident, but not cocky. Basically, you're playing you, to varying degrees. And the real you is what they need to see. We get as many as 30,000 submissions for some of these commercials. You need to show them why it should be you. Your uniqueness is really all you have."

This is fine on its face, but it ignores the fact that there are thousands of other people being their real selves, too. One of them will get the job, for myriad reasons that likely have nothing to do with what they showed them in that room, reasons that may not even include their face or body. It's easy to feel like if you don't get the gig, you must have failed to be you. You weren't *you* enough, you see.

Don't forget the money that's at stake. The costs of these projects are staggering; no one can risk all that on an unknown. Add to that the fact that the people in the audition room have no real power and no imagination, are only playing their own role in this ridiculous farce — the harried assistant, immovable executive, fearful minion, the unhinged fill-in-the-blank — and well, you're not getting cast. The safest way for them to do their job is to hire someone who has done something very similar if not exactly like this already. For example, if they need a woman with curly brown hair, they're going to go with the woman with curly brown hair they already know.

That's an inside joke. See, what's funny is that they never cast anyone with curly brown hair.

That's why you see the same people in so many commercials. People say they don't want to be typecast, but you're very lucky if that happens to you. You'll be able to tell yourself you have that immutable *something*.

At least some of the people in the audition room enjoy their power and love making other people jump through hoops. What they want is entirely subjective and unknowable to me. And that's why being me is as good a choice as any. But I choke. There's no way they want this desperate, anxious, depressed person. And there's no way that these days of seeing hundreds of actors for this tiny part in an internet-only, thirty-second commercial that will run for two weeks is anything but show. That's the real theater. The whole house of cards depends on this charade. The collective dreams of actors everywhere fund the whole thing. So here we all are.

If your real you isn't full of resentment and anger, if your real you isn't distracted with worry about being late getting back to work or getting a parking ticket, then go for it. It's a shot in the dark. The hard truth is that no matter how *you* you manage to be, any number of people could do a good job at this thing. You'll either win the lottery or convince yourself to buy another ticket. Reset your hopes and dreams, sign up for another class.

When I'd committed, as much as I was able, to getting my piece of the commercial casting pie, I paid for a one-on-one coaching class with him. Here he would record my work and share it with people he knew in The Industry. I had no reason to doubt him, as he was a prominent casting agent and seemed sincere about liking my work. But it was a very safe impression for him to give. If nothing came of it, well, that's Hollywood. It would certainly not be because he never did what he promised.

In any case, a few weeks after the one-on-one class, a friend asked if I'd heard back from him about our session and if there was any feedback from his contacts. And since I hadn't, she convinced me to write to him and follow up. I was reticent, but she said, and she was right, that it's not only reasonable to follow up, but expected. This is how The Industry works. I wrote, and his rapid and condescending reply advised patience with a thinly veiled subtext of *how dare you, I'm in charge here.* I never heard from him again.

It's for each of us to decide to be part of all this or not. Some actors build a tough outer shell. Others are covered in scars. And still others protect themselves, and make a trade they don't realize they're making. They just never get those headshots taken; they don't go to auditions. They stay safe.

Tough Enough

ALL THE RULES WE accept about the best way to succeed were written by gatekeepers. We usually don't have a choice but to play by their changing, sometimes dangerous rules, but it's all a trap. There's a vested interest in making sure very few people get through the door in Hollywood, even while the whole enterprise depends on selling the idea that anyone can.

"You need to be tough," and "If you can't stand the heat," etc. It's the water we swim in. Lots of people, I'm sure, think they'll just play the game for a little while, just till they get in the door. But there's always another door.

There are people trying to do good work, trying to advance their careers, trying to make a living. And there are others who are actively making all that harder than it has to be. It's okay to hit a limit.

"The elephant doesn't have a thick enough skin," the big-game hunter says as he hoists the elephant gun onto his shoulder.

I can see now what a terrible mistake I made. But I've always wanted to win against the odds. I wanted someone to find me, value what was mostly hidden. That was the proof I was looking for.

It bothers me that the What it Takes argument, at its core, advocates for a homogenous pool of very tough customers. Only people of a certain personality and temperament can pass through, and that makes things so very samey and boring. It makes things mostly male and almost entirely white. It excludes lots of people, so many might-have-beens. Every single person who couldn't "make it," who didn't pass the shifting litmus test, had something to offer. The best art in the world is vulnerable, but there's very little space made for those artists, and we can't get there uninjured. And you know what? People who are impervious to pain — those tough enough — are seldom thoughtful or generous artists. They are often sociopaths.

There is case after case of awful people doing terrible things to other people, and those awful people may go away for a while, but they'll be back. They are back, they move through the system virtually unfettered, but still aggrieved and mostly unrepentant. At any audition, table read, or film shoot, there's a good chance you will have to interact with a terrible, if not dangerous, person. You'll be forced to fawn over someone who ought to be in jail, whether you know it or not. If everything goes well, you might even have to do press tours with that person, you might have to one day post a video apology to your socials for your seeming support of a living piece of shit.

Everyone assesses their own risk, and almost all will hit a limit eventually. That they have a lower threshold for this nonsense doesn't make them worse than the one who stays. It's a rigged game, set up for this outcome exactly, but that won't stop those speechifying about how to play it better. Gah, save us from armchair athletes.

It's easy math, in the end. Please stop lecturing people on how they need to be in order to get through the door you're standing in front of. The decisions to move on or out aren't about cowardice or toughness. They're about return on investment. Why stay where terrible people and their enablers are in charge? You'll call it weakness, and we're all made to feel like that's what it is, but it's an act of strength to refuse to play the game. You know this, but if you act like it's all very fair and aboveboard, then we are obviously emotional, unreasonable, overreacting. Talk about unoriginal stories, my goodness, I'm sick of it.

You'll say it toughens me up, that my work is better for the struggle. But I balk at thanking my abusers for all the amazing benefits I am reaping, all the wonderful ways I'm resilient now.

This decision to remove oneself from an unsafe space is somehow a failure of one's dedication to art and not an indictment of the entire system. Our only choice is between staying and going, and you still can't even give us that? *Why didn't they just leave?* turns into *How could they have left?* in a second, and you don't even hear yourselves. We're just doing as you said, but now we know there will be no respect for us no matter what we choose.

I've always told my story as one of someone with a host of issues preventing her getting through. Who didn't have the drive or the confidence, none of it entirely untrue, but there was something else at work: fear. My physical and emotional safety was clearly at risk, and I could not overcome my anxieties. I knew my creative self couldn't withstand what was being dished out. I am geared to make myself vulnerable, that's my offering. In a different world, I think I might have been able to contribute something. But throwing myself over wall after wall in hopes of getting through to people who don't give a shit about what I create, and in fact, are just playing a game they have a vested interest in me losing? No. Again, it's the freaking wizard. Bring you the broomstick? Here, let me shove it up your ass.

Bit Part: Mouthing the Words

I AM ABSOLUTELY TERRIFIED of singing in public. It's a hundred percent related to my body dysmorphic disorder, and I can't control it. Not the phobia, obviously, but I also can't control my voice at all if I think anyone might be listening and judging. Because everyone listening is judging. I wince at other people's sour notes too, but my fear of causing that wince in others is outsized. It's a reflection on me as a person, a clear-as-a-bell failure in flat notes.

There's a special sort of glee in the exposure of a bad singer; it's something everyone can join in on. I don't think mine is a particularly interesting voice in the end, so this isn't a tragedy, but if I could sing well, I wouldn't do anything else.

It certainly would have helped me professionally. I was once reduced to tears in an audition for a children's theater because they asked me to sing "Happy Birthday." I was famous in grad school for my lip-synching abilities (you gotta hit your plosives).

I used to be able to sing when I was relaxed, like when I was with people whose love I felt secure in. But even that is mostly gone now; my issues have not improved with age. Everyone promised I'd wear purple damn hats and stop caring about what others think, but for me, in some ways it only gets worse. I was worried about my face when it was youthful and unlined, I'm exponentially more so now.

Obviously, I'm even worse at dancing.

That's it, folks. Single-threat actor over here, who can do comedy (make 'em laugh *on purpose*, that's key) and not much else. Hollywood, here I come! You're not going to know what hit you. Literally, I mean. You'll never know I was there.

Yes, And

WITHIN THE FIRST YEAR after I moved to LA, a friend, a transplant I'd known from Chicago, convinced me to begin classes with her at bang. improv studio, on Fairfax. Improv was booming and there were lots of schools to choose from, but most of them came with gatekeepers I knew I would never challenge. The vibe at bang. was warm and inviting, and after graduation, almost two years later, I happily stuck around, deepening my relationships with wonderful people and doing good, funny work in as safe a creative space as I'd ever known. It was a tremendous gift.

Improv is good for everyone. The basic skills you'll learn are good no matter what you do for a living: eye contact, listening, staying present, taking care of your partner. Like therapy, it's also enormously informative, if you're willing to do the work. If, for example, listening is a problem for you in improv, it's probably an issue you could stand to address in your real life. Do you interrupt your improv partner? Do you take over scenes? Do you hang back and let others lead? You probably do all of this in real life, too. I said no a lot in life, and I wanted to try out this yes thing. Not just yes. Yes *and*.

It can be scary to head out onto the stage without a plan. But here are a few more nuggets you can easily apply to everything: You're not alone. You may not have a clear map for what's to come, but you do have tools. No one is sent out without training. Improv isn't magic; it's about being prepared, trusting yourself and others, and watching for opportunities.

It's good to push yourself a little, and you may think that feeling that fear is the whole lesson, but the more valuable part for me is that failure is survivable. The worst thing that can happen in an improv set isn't bad, or unforgivable, or even noteworthy. Nothing really happens when you fail at improv. You might lose a little sleep over a bad show, but you'll be fine, I promise. For someone with an anxiety disorder, this realization was revelatory.

When you succeed? Well, that's some heady shit. There's nothing like a roomful of people laughing together because of something you said or did or created. It's like nothing else in the world. It's a potent drug.

It's not all roses. I remember an evening running a workout for a few groups who would be performing a few days later, some for the very first time. And in the middle of individual games of zip-zap-zup, one young woman peeled off from her group and rushed up to me. "I can't stand these people," she whispered, in some panic. "What do I do?"

They were to perform together each week for the next six months. I told her to decide she loved them. Act like they were family — weird and annoying but loved — and that she only had to do it for the time they'd be working together. I only had a few seconds to come up with something, and I don't know if it worked or was even good advice. It just seemed that even conflicted love was a better launching pad than hate. *Say yes.* Finding a healthy way to deal with people you don't like very much is another life skill.

There's a lot of talk in improv to "follow the fear." Embrace the discomfort. That wasn't easy for me, partly because I don't like feeling uncomfortable, but even more, I don't want to make other people uncomfortable. I'm also reluctant to put an audience through anything I wouldn't like if I was in the audience. But that's a long list, so I did have to push myself.

The sense of accomplishment when you jump over the improv hurdle bleeds into the rest of your life. *What are you afraid of, Jenny? Go for it! Get out of your comfort zone!* You end up convincing yourself that the thing you don't want to do will be a fun adventure. It works well for some stuff, but I wasn't sure how to tell when I just didn't want to do something. Do I have to follow every fear? Surely my screaming self-preservation instincts should occasionally win the day.

Generally, though, it's a good lesson. Stretch yourself.

Alas, I philosophize better than I improvise. I was good but not great. I was too stuck in my head, too literal and lateral a thinker to be really inventive about world-building. And I was so concerned about letting my partner do what they wanted to do that I failed to contribute enough or give good gifts, which in the end isn't really supporting them well at all. My strength, weirdly, was patience. I was fine with silence. I could wait for the scene to reveal itself, to let it build slowly, and not let panic lead me to go for cheap laughs. Earned laughs are so, so much more gratifying. Totally worth the wait. The best, heartiest laughs you give an audience are almost never jokes. And I don't mean that's all there is. The riveted, rapt silences are cool, too. There's a huge amount of trust in those silences. The audience is not your enemy, they're part of the show.

Were there moments of brilliance? Yes! AND, that's true for everyone who has spent time trying to do improv well.

Success probably hinges on whether you can see the next thing as frightening or just a mystery. What would it be like to anticipate the next thing with curiosity rather than trepidation? I spent a lot of my regular life in reaction mode, braced for what was coming rather than interested in what it would bring. And it was a normal place to land. But it took so long to put my head back up. On stage, and in life, it's all about how you react. Do you accept what's given and add something good, or sit and wish it had been different? It's probably the main difference between a great show and an okay show. I would really like to have a great show.

Renouncing My Claim to Fame

I RECENTLY FOUND AN old essay called "Hollywood Manifesto," in which I wrote about my hope that I could still, despite my age, reach one or two of my goals with respect to the movie industry and the pursuit of an artistic sort of life. In it, I argue that as a mature adult with a sense of humor, a low number on the eccentric dial, and some skills in various areas, I might be a good choice for casting, maybe in a movie, be it teleplay or feature film.

I've also long clung to the idea that I could be a writer, maybe of a movie, be it teleplay or feature film. I thought I was lucky, having not one but two areas for potential success.

This wasn't so very long ago, but I already have an update. I am giving up. I give up.

Say you're buying a house, and you decide at the beginning of the process that it absolutely needs to be a three-bedroom, two-and-a-half bath Colonial, on at least a half-acre in a rural community, within reasonable driving distance of a decent-sized city, preferably a tertiary market. You begin your search full of hope, sure that if you just keep looking, you'll find everything you want within your price range. As you go, you realize that a two-plus-two ranch-style house in the suburbs with a decent yard would do just as well, as long as it's on a quiet street or cul-de-sac. And then you go even farther down the path, and you think a busier thoroughfare would be alright, if it's set back from the street and there's some defensive landscaping, and — bottom line — has one bedroom and a den. So it goes, until you end up somehow sharing a condo that's backed up to a highway, but it's not too bad because there are no windows on that side of the building.

You didn't give up on your dreams, you just had to whittle them down to an almost unrecognizable nub. This is how I feel about my life right now. I can map out the steep and steady descent.

I've wanted to act since I was a very little girl, but that's all I have for you. I don't have stories about classes and recitals, or the elaborate shows I'd put on for the neighbors. I didn't do any of that. My desire to act was, for whatever reason, my secret, but I felt rather strongly that it was my destiny, that it was meant to be. I identified with two areas where you're supposed to self-proclaim, acting and writing. I showed no early signs of talent for either of those things, but I felt pulled to them. That seemed at least to be a prerequisite.

My struggle to write started in eighth grade, during a Creative Writing elective. In what would become a lifelong pattern, I thought, "Yes. That's it. That's it." I had no idea what I was doing, but I knew I wanted to be good at it. In what would become a lifelong pattern, I learned that the class was for fully formed Creative Writers. It was not for people who wanted to be taught how to write creatively, or, as in my case, wanted to know what that phrase even meant. I had no way of knowing going in. As early as junior high, apparently, you can run into that wall: "Some things can't be taught." That's what the so-called experts like to hear themselves say, but that doesn't mean they won't take your money for the class. Arriving fully formed is an issue of mine, and I think it dates to the C that I got in that class, that damning C.

If that class had started with the idea that the students were already creative, it would have been about teaching me that was true, and would have revealed and discovered my talents, filled in the gaps with technique, and built the confidence I needed to pursue greatness. This may be a lot to ask of an 8th grade elective, and I'm not saying we were all geniuses. I get that talent is a factor outside all of this, but what if you're 12 and you don't even have the basic vocabulary? Please, show me the bones. If I walk into Algebra 101, no one asks me first thing to find x.

I was looking for something I wasn't going to get. I was expected to already know what I was, with or without proof or training. And it must work, because if you look around, there are plenty of people making a tidy living writing or acting and there's no proof that they can do either. (Hey, I said I'd given up, not that I wasn't still angry about it.)

A year after I got that C, bruised but not beaten, I confided in two friends my brand-new plan to write the story of my life. Big words from a ninth grader, and yes, absurd and funny. At least, they thought so. Oh, how they laughed. I don't think either of them had ever heard anything so hilarious. When they were finished, we all wiped tears away. But this was instructive: keep your dreams to yourself. Unfortunately, this runs counter to the accepted philosophies about winning and getting what you want. You have to put it out there, they'll say. You gotta believe.

Never mind that we were in ninth grade, or that it would take me 25 years to pick up a pen, or that writing the story of my life, in these small increments, is exactly what I'm doing. None of that matters because I can't make a living.

My favorite star interview is when the very famous actress, spawned by very famous actors, producers or directors, explains that her success is due to how very hard she worked. Every door was open to her, but she thinks the playing field was level, or at least wants you to believe that it was. She may be talented, and she probably does work very hard, but you see what I'm saying. It's like a lottery winner telling me I just didn't want it enough.

The person who got cast in the big part may have given the best audition of her life, but because you gave the best audition of your life does not mean you'll be cast. The best thing you ever wrote will not necessarily be published, though many first-time published authors will tell you it was their best thing ever — they are going to say that because it was published. Because you love someone with your whole heart doesn't mean they will return those feelings. Each of these things seem like the key to the puzzle, but they are only one part. They are prerequisites, not guarantees.

Every winner will tell you that persistence is a major part of their success. Good for you, Successful Person, you stuck to it. Kudos. I know why it ends up at the top of your list of how you did it, but don't forget that the rest is alchemy. I get that you have to play to win. But there are lots of us who play our hearts out and still lose.

I'm not saying you should stop trying, but just don't turn around once you've made it and pretend hanging in there is the one weird trick. Don't slap our shiny, hopeful faces.

As with that dream house, I have whittled down my list. I gave up on any sort of success and fortune as it relates to writing and acting, and my list now consists of writing freelance web content from my crappy rental house in North Hollywood. And it's become clear I'm not going to get that, either.

Perhaps I can add those other things back in one day. But I'll never be able to say, "I never gave up hope." Because I did, I do, I have.

I've modified my dream acceptance speech accordingly:

Kids! I had very little help and I wasn't born into money. I gave up on my dreams all the time. I needed to make a living, and perhaps most importantly, I lacked confidence in what I was doing, got very little encouragement early on, and possessed none of the requisite skills like hustling and asking for stuff. Hell, yeah, I gave up, often and for sometimes long stretches of time. I traded almost anything on my list for the basic necessities of food and shelter. I took a succession of jobs that meant nothing to me, but still actively avoided learning new skills or climbing any ladder, because I thought I was meant for something Big. Which is ridiculous. I was wrong. In fairness, I did work my ass off, but in the end, it wasn't for anything I really wanted, just the life things that I really needed — do not *play me off, Mr. Conductor, I'm almost done. Dreams do come true, kids, for .00000002 percent of people. I am living proof of that. Thank you, and good night!*

Bit Part: Win and Lose

Growing up in my house with my unpredictable mother, I did everything I could to make sure she didn't get mad at me. It's an old story — be the perfect child and escape the wrath, in whatever form that took. It worked, but it backfired on me when I felt my parents start to favor me over my sisters. As an adult I fight hard to be the best/most liked/whatever, and then I'm consumed with guilt when I'm pulled up and out of the crowd. A good review for the show I'm in is great; if it highlights my work specifically, I want to die.

Circle of Life

WHEN I FIRST GOT to LA, I temped. I'd done it a few times before, and though the work was never steady, I'd occasionally get a receptionist gig or a data entry something. One of my early assignments was for an obscure company that provided promotional items to companies: keychains, koozies. I was installed at the front desk on my first day, an eager, would-be starlet, living the dream, answering phones.

Someone had mentioned that the married owners were coming in. To my surprise, the husband was a very recognizable actor who had been on an extremely popular TV show when I was a teenager, a police procedural that made him very well known, if only briefly.

I wasn't starstruck, but I was surprised and sort of delighted, having only been in town for a little while. But it's not like I saw him on TV anymore, or at least not very often. I took it in as a lesson. When and if something good happens — your gritty drama takes off, ushering in countless other gritty dramas — save and invest your money in a real-world business that can sustain you. He'd obviously done exactly that, and didn't need to worry if the auditions weren't exactly pouring in. He was a very particular type and it was a smart move. The office was not fancy, off the beaten path, but the company had a huge catalog, and I wouldn't be surprised if it's still going strong.

Years and years later, I went with a friend to a play in a mall theater in Burbank, and there he was, acting. In a play. In a mall theater in Burbank, but still! And again, honestly, I was impressed. He was still at it, wasn't he? He was acting when he could, doing his work, making it work.

It's the circle of life in Hollywood. When the show hits big, it's easy to think it is just the beginning, the first of many. But it might be the end. It might be the only show. For everyone on the red carpet, there are thousands of us slogging away, temping, investing, hungry, dreaming. Good for him for being clear-eyed. One may dream of doing amazing things, but one should be prepared to make do with what comes along.

This is the kind of thing I should have been doing, I berated myself before the lights went down. Stay at it, do the work, feed yourself — get paid, yes, but *do the work*. I used to say it in grad school when challenged about the future. "What if you don't make it?" It depends on what your definition of that is. It doesn't have to be about fame and fortune. I just wanted to work. I don't know when I got off course.

My god, it was a terrible play. He was good in it, because he's a good actor, but oof. (My friend's review as we beelined for her car: "I feel like I've been attacked.")

An actor can be great in the audition and even better in the role, but the material might still be terrible. So, so much of what is produced here is just ... not good. Still, if you're an actor who wants to work, then you fit yourself into that. Swallow your pride and whatever expectations you might have had, and make it work for you. That's the lesson. Keep showing up. If you can stand it.

73% There

WITH SO LITTLE ACTING experience under my belt at the end of college, I decided to pursue an MFA. I thought it would be the best route for me to get more experience, and this bore out, but I was a constant disappointment to many of my professors. I was repeatedly urged to "jump off the cliff," a note at once so vague and so threatening as to be completely paralyzing.

I mean, I sort of understood what they meant, just not how to do it. I was a contained sort of actor with an as-yet-undiagnosed fear of a certain kind of physical exposure. I couldn't throw myself around a stage without a well-articulated reason and a clear understanding of what exactly was expected from me. I couldn't guess at it, and they were not always helpful. I maintain, some 30-plus years later, that "just go for it" and "jump off the cliff" are not good notes. One of the people in charge of our collective fates would regularly say about our scene work, "It's about 73% there."

I could only meet them part way when it came to the broad theatricality they seemed to want. Once, I was doing a Shakespeare scene and my character, arguing with someone, starts to leave the room but then changes her mind. My professor wanted me to grab the stage curtains in my hands on the way out, fists shaking, then visibly calm myself and resolve to return. I still don't think I was entirely wrong to resist that schlocky garbage, but I couldn't even fake it for the sake of the grade. I felt ridiculous. I felt like I *looked* ridiculous.

The conclusion was that I was a more subtle actor, better suited to the screen. Haha.

When you're starting out, there are a few things you tell yourself. You just want to make a living at this, you only want to hone your craft and get better with each project. That message is hammered into you in grad school, too, with additions: *Don't expect success, this is a hard path,* etc. But there was a subtext, too, one impossible to ignore, impossible not to be seduced by. *You are one of the dedicated ones. Resilient, special.*

Also: *teach this class, build that set.*

All the emphasis was about what we lacked rather than what we had. For all the emphasis on what the "real world" would be like, they missed this one by a mile. No one in the real world expects me to be good at everything, they only need me to be very good at one to three things. For years I tried out for every serious play I could find, because I didn't give my natural tendency toward comedy any credit at all. Comedy came easier, so I didn't respect it. But I wish I had. I wish they'd told me, *This is your thing, Jenny, and it's okay to claim it.*

They should have taught me how to market my particular talents, the real thing, my unique me-ness. It was their job — at least a part of it — to help me figure out how to make a living at this. I get that you should push your limits, yes. But I submit that no one stands up on stage and does anything they aren't willing to do, whether that's humping a fake horse while naked or a soft-shoe dance routine.

The world isn't served when we all do the same exact thing. My teachers spent so much time and effort trying to get us to a neutral place, a blank slate, so that we could then morph into anything. But that wasn't something anyone in the real world wanted. It's like the classic complaint about high school algebra — we're never going to need this.

Another favorite phrase was, "Here, we break you down, then we build you back up." If you hear this, *run*. The person who said it is pre-excusing shitty behavior. It's not a method, it's an excuse. Half the time, they don't even know what they mean.

You can say anything with authority when you present it as a life lesson. These same people told the three women in my class that they needed to lose 5, 10 and 15 pounds, respectively — and yes, I won, I was the one who needed to lose 15 pounds. This message was delivered through a female movement teacher from the dean and artistic director, both men. Mind you, I was maybe 140 pounds when I got that note, and I did not find it helpful in the least. I let them know this was a sure way for me to gain more, and that I and the other women in the class — who were both much slimmer than me — agreed that they might want to lay the fuck off about our weight. It was just so cliché, and I think that's what I resented the most. It was ironic that they exhorted us to be more real when they were such caricatures. Such ridiculous stereotypes.

After all this emphasis on doing everything well, and the clear message that I couldn't do much of anything at all, the idea that I should also be more revealing of myself was infuriating. The only thing I knew for sure was that they didn't like how I looked; nothing was ever going to come from a jaded professor saying, "More, Jenny." Creating a safe place for me to work is literally the very least you can do. Figure out what you want from me and how to communicate that — it's your actual job.

I don't think these folks were the right people for me. It's not the first or last time that happened, but I do recognize that it wasn't just them. We were all outmatched by my demons, unbeknownst to us all.

We need actors with different skill sets, different thresholds. Which brings me back to the naked actor who's faking sex with the horse — I'm referring to a character in *Equus*, by Peter Shaffer — lots of people maybe wouldn't want to do that, but that actor is okay with it. And it doesn't make him better or worse than the next guy. He might also think that baring your soul to total strangers is too scary a thing to contemplate. To him, I'm the bravest person in town. Well, maybe 73% there.

Agency

THE COMMERCIAL ACTING CLASS I took resulted in an interested agent, and we worked together, if it can be called that, for six or eight months before he severed our relationship with an actual mailed letter. I had failed to produce new headshots from among the list of photographers he'd suggested, and he considered this an indicator that I was not as serious about my path as he was. I considered it an indicator that I'd been unemployed for the entirety of our relationship.

I was once told that there are 100,000 people just like me being submitted for roles, per hour. That seems impossible — the volume and the timeline, yes, but mainly the just like me part. Come on. You keep telling me there's no one like me. But you also keep telling me what's wrong with me, you keep trying to squeeze me into a box. You keep telling me it must be my headshots.

I also have to wonder how it's meant to be inspiring. My answer to that, for good or ill, is "They can have it." I was never taught to compete, so there's that, but I also know a rigged game when I see one. And their arguments assume that me-as-me is something anyone wants to hire. We're all just guessing, and I am sick of it. Maybe this is the downside to starting out so late, but I choose to see it as a benefit. I'm not going to jump through your hoops. I could break a hip.

I needed to be seen as different and unique, and they wanted me to be the same as everyone else. At least, that's how it felt. It was the opposite of what I needed, an unresolvable tension. Of course I didn't get anywhere. I was in the wrong where, viscerally opposed to erasing myself, shitting in the wrong pot.

At a party around that time, I was seated directly across from the only person at the table I didn't know. And eventually it came out that I was a performer, and he asked about what I was doing, and I confessed not much. And he launched into a monologue about self-sabotage and what might be holding me back. I could hardly form my argument about being me and having fun and not running someone else's play. He was perfectly friendly, but intense on the subject, and I got the idea that this was a speech he needed to hear more than I did. It was a speech he'd said a lot.

His argument was that you must do whatever you have to, even if that's to step in line with the thousands of others doing the same thing. As someone who grapples with issues about being seen and noticed, that seems like the most self-sabotaging thing I could do. He said he'd "given up a lot to come here," whereas I'm unwilling to give up anything at all. I don't have much, but that probably explains it. I'm going to protect this tiny pile, thank you very much. Of course, once the issue of self-sabotage is introduced, nothing you say to explain yourself sounds like anything but that. I changed the subject. Mine is not a popular view or even a defensible one. I'm doomed to fail, even though I'm trying so hard to do what they say. Be myself.

Bit Part: Can You Hear Me Now?

SPARE A THOUGHT FOR the popular spokesperson on television, the one who scored the multi-year deal that includes billboards, mailings, and internet banner ads — that person was probably a trained actor with a set of specific, now impossible, goals. They are now rich, no doubt, but also virtually un-castable. Their dreams probably died the day they signed the contract, though they may not have known it. This is someone who — like literally all of us — was sold the idea that they should add commercials to their body of work. The money isn't what it once was in most cases, but it can nicely supplement your day job. It can pay for the headshots you need to re-do every 18 months. It can give you a sense that you're on the right track, and you were right to stick it out, that this commercial will naturally lead to bigger and better things. This is seldom true, but the real business of Hollywood is to sell possibility, to feed those dreams. It has a vested interest in the maximum number of people possible thinking they will be the ones to crack the code.

In any case, that person probably couldn't see that far into the future. So many of these campaigns are short-lived. But some have legs. Some stick around for years. They couldn't have known that when they signed the contract. But they were, I can almost promise you, tired. Tired of living lean or bouncing checks. Tired of not being able to fly home at the holidays, of avoiding regular doctor visits. Tired of auditions. Tired of waiting.

Going Solo

DURING THIS LONG STRETCH in LA when I say I did nothing, I did write and produce a one-person show. It was entirely about my love of romance novels and the things that love brings up in me and in people who learn this fact about me. My elevator pitch to total strangers goes like this: It's about why I love romance novels and why your opinion of me just shifted over if not down.

It is, in a larger sense, also about why we love what we love, and where that might have come from. That we all need a form of escape, and we find different routes, and that my way is no better or worse than yours. Why it's so important that we let ourselves have these things.

Writing the show took forever, which is to say, the usual amount of time. I found a director and wasted a lot of her time and my money working through it until I finally launched it.

In the end, as always, I was looking forward to being done. I maybe waited a bit too long. The doing of it was still fun, but everything else really wore on me. Lugging props across town, setting up and striking, promotion, printing programs ... it was a lot. I suppose it would be different if I'd had more help, which is usually the way of things. And it would be nice if all that work came to anything in the end.

I have had this persistent belief that if you do the best you can on work that really means something to you, it will lead to the next thing. Not necessarily a Big Huge Thing, but something. The next step would be revealed. I might be approached about a larger venue, a manager, a small role in another project.

It hasn't happened that way. And I think that as a rule, I tend to abandon the effort, even when it is a worthwhile one. I have a weird ability, once I've come to terms with the disappointment, to let it go and move on even when that means starting back at zero. I sort of hope that's not the case here, but I guess it's fine if it is. I really am proud of what I've done, but what difference does that really make? When do you just call it and head off in a new direction?

I was complaining about all this a while back, and a friend asked what I'd expected. It was an honest question, although in my sensitivity, I may have heard a bit of an accusatory tone. I'd hoped the same thing I always hope: to be noticed, acknowledged. And that it would come with a prize. She also asked if I was proud of myself, and I am. It didn't come easy. Little old, hide-your-light me, glacial follower and then abandoner of dreams, put on a show. Her Royal Highness of Reluctance *put on a show*. And it happens that it's funny and people like it. Fuck, yes, I'm proud of myself. There aren't that many things I'm prouder of.

But ... gosh, it was such a lot of work. If I'd had any more money to throw at it, I'd have hired a stage manager maybe. If I were another person entirely, I might have, you know, asked for help.

Sidenote: My props included about 200 paperback romance novels. I started to obsess on the commute to and from the theater about being in an accident and seeing them all strewn across the

405. Can you imagine the headlines? I can. I would have to die in that accident. It would be the only way to live it down.

It's strange, but knowing as I do how difficult it was to get it done, it still feels — now that I'm on the other side — that it wasn't very much at all. Which is odd. Maybe it would feel bigger if something more came out of it.

All that straining for such a tiny poop.

I've decided to relaunch the show as a living-room concept, with me at a lectern and my slides on the TV. I've always wanted it to be more portable, and of course I'm a fan of anything where my body moves around less. My hope is that it will grow organically. A guest at the first show would want to do it at their house. And so on. Like Tupperware sales, but for salon-style entertainment.

This show is the bravest thing I have ever done, but it doesn't follow that there will be a prize for that. Funny that that's what the show is about — the stories we're told about what to expect and the things we do to fill in the gap between what we were promised and what we got. I guess that's today's revelation. I got caught in the same old trap. And it doesn't matter that I know there are no guarantees, that I'm old enough to have seen that again and again. Part of me still believes. Some little kid in me still thinks hard work is rewarded and things you make from your bleeding heart will change the world.

The subject matters to me. I want to talk about it. I want to share it. Which is how I got this far at all. But am I right about it being worth sharing? What does any of it matter in the end?

I'm acting like everyone needs to love this show. They don't. I know that's impossible, and I know it's not necessary to it being a success. The issues have less to do with them and more with me.

I know I'm working with and against serious mental obstacles. There is no part of this that isn't difficult for me. But that is the part that people really don't want to hear about. The artist should make art, and if they are going whine about it the whole time ... well, I can see how little patience people have for that. I want to stop being that person who won't shut up about how little she believes in herself. But on the other hand — talking about the icky stuff is what I do. This problem is just so unattractive.

I am underconfident. It sucks. It makes me discard decent ideas, judge the ones I do pursue, and doubt the results. And none of that is interesting. You might as well talk about the traffic on the way over, how your cold is progressing, or why you were late. It's boring. And anyway, there's nothing to be done about it. In the end, I'm asking to be given something I'm incapable of accepting. I'm wasting everyone's time.

It's the same vibe I get when I try to talk about how lonely I sometimes feel. Another solo effort. There's a tightening of the features, like they are girding themselves to not say the things that need saying. *Suck it up. Figure it out. Shut up already.*

I picked a subject — love and romance — that is painful in the extreme, even while it's my favorite thing to talk about. Is it good enough? Funny enough? Too serious? Am I too naked, and if so ... um, how do I look naked? Am I wasting my time? Will I survive this? Will anyone care if I don't?

I don't know. It could be that this show will not get very far at all, that I'll barely break even, that I'll fold it up and put it away and move on. But maybe not. No matter what happens, I will have done it. It's the minimum prize, absolutely guaranteed. And that's not bad for last place.

Stage Five:

Consolation

What You Need to Do

Advice, even when it's truly well-meaning, isn't usually about what you should do. It's about what the person doling out the advice would do. It doesn't take you into account very often, I find. I call people who give this advice youneeders, as in, "You need to do this" or "You know what you need to do ...."

Unfortunately, the only way forward is to figure out for yourself the things you're capable of doing and then to pick from the ones you're willing to put effort toward.

Statistically speaking, everyone who ever won an award and was asked for advice says something like, "You can be anything you want to be." This is patently untrue. It's the laziest kind of pabulum offered by someone who has never stopped to think about what the real secret of their success might be.

I'm a little tired of the post-game analyses. It seems that a disproportionately small number of these people have any real idea how it happened for them, or how much of it was luck.

Honestly, if someone were to pluck me off the street today and put me in a small, plum role (the chubby, sarcastic, curly-haired, friend-slash-coworker) and the movie took off and got real attention, there would be a small part of me whispering, "I knew it. I *knew* it." And also, "I never gave up."

Those dreams don't die, maybe because we've been fed a steady diet of this kind of thing — rags to riches, baby. Never give up.

But that's not how it happens. I can't count the number of times I've given up. I probably shouldn't have in every case, but there were times when it was appropriate and even necessary.

Again (ad nauseam), we're sold a lot of stories. I can neither sing nor dance. If I could do either, I wouldn't do anything else. And you can say, take classes! Devote yourself! But I am here to tell you, with the wisdom of all my years on this planet and in this body, that no amount of singing and dancing lessons would make me a good singer or dancer. And that's okay — or it ought to be. We can't all be everything.

If you are a woman of a certain age and still hoping to make a living acting, you'll have heard that story about that one actress who moved to Hollywood when she was in her mid-50s and was cast in a bunch of things. She had a recurring role for the first couple of seasons in a popular TV series, then was killed off because of the promise of a bigger role in another show that I don't think ever happened.

I used to hear about her a lot. She's dead now, but the story still occasionally makes the rounds on social media. And it's a great story. She made changes in a life she was unsatisfied with, and she got lucky — a vital piece of the puzzle. She wanted to do it, and she did it, and I give her all due respect. Don't give up on your dreams, kids!

But I don't like it when clear exceptions to the rule are held up as some sort of inspiration because they are, if anything, the opposite.

Stop talking about the one person who managed to slip in the door and start focusing on why so many of the doors are shut.

It's hard to accept advice from people at the top. It's all fine on its face, but it's usually offered by people who don't have a particular problem with any of it, or who are insulated from caring because they are sitting on a pile of money and surrounded by awards.

Don't depend on others for validation, that's a fun one. How on earth do you not depend on others for validation, when an actor's entire career is about exactly that? If you mean that you need to be unattached to the results of your efforts, then you are likely one of those people with an independent income and you have no business advising those of us at the bottom.

I realize if it's hard to accept advice from those at the top, it will be impossible to accept it from someone at the bottom. And I can see why, if given a choice between "Don't give up" and "You should definitely give up," most of us listen to the former. I don't want to discourage the hopeful; you should persevere, if that is what makes sense for you. But if it doesn't feel quite right, if it hasn't fed you in the way you thought it would, if you've wondered if you're on the right path, then there is no shame in moving onto another. We are all so different. What if giving up is the exact right choice? What if a whole different world awaits?

To be clear, I gave up on the dream in my head. I had never, not once, given it an appropriate amount of focus in real life. If you're in the fight, if you're hustling for an agent and going on auditions and retaking those headshots, I applaud you. I couldn't do it.

The winners are right that you need to believe in yourself, because the whole thing is soul-sucking. We are, in almost all things, totally reliant on other people, and other people are just people. Human beings as flawed and flailing as the rest of us. "Let all that roll off you," the winners say from their mansions in the hills, while you cry your way to work.

"You need to tell the Universe what you want," is another gem, very popular in Hollywood. It's also offered by people who haven't thought about their success, who haven't stared with any clarity into that abyss. It galls me, not only because it's facile, but because it's absolutely not the secret to any kind of artistic success. Let me tell you, whispering your secret yearnings to an empty room has no effect whatsoever on outcomes here. On this, I am an expert.

I know we're trying to make sense of what doesn't make sense, but can we find a way to do it that doesn't insult me to my core? I didn't ask for any of this. I remember distinctly asking for completely different stuff.

I'm not against the idea in principle. Being clear about what you want is valuable. But thinking it will come to you because you've "put it out there" is disingenuous.

Yes, I'm a bone-deep cynic. I'm sorry. I spent a lot of time wishing and hoping, and saying it out loud at a range of volumes. I wish someone had told me how to add in all the hard work, how to not be the perverse weirdo who refuses to toe the prescribed line, who balks at the gate.

Turning myself into a cookie-cutter version of everyone else in this town doesn't feel like self-worth to me. Going back again and again on auditions, begging for someone to just read an essay, wishing an agent would believe in me, none of that makes me feel good about myself. The truth is, your best work may very well be great, but that doesn't mean someone else couldn't do it just as well. Differently, sure, uniquely their own. But equally well.

There's a fundamental imbalance here: the art doesn't need any of us as much as we need the art. Maybe that's why none of it really satisfies, why so few actors ever really retire. We love something that can't really love us back.

This isn't a prescription. It isn't an indictment. We can't all be successful at this, that's all. It isn't feasible or even necessary. It's fine to give up. It has to be. And I don't mean that you should. Only that I need to.

The Way Life Should Be

IMAGINE YOUR PERSONAL WORST-CASE scenario for your old age, then multiply that by ten. That's the hand my dad was dealt. I'd been getting reports from my sisters, who both live closer and make more regular trips to see him, and those reports were alarming enough to get me to Maine.

Goodness, I'm a basket case. There were many hurdles — financial, logistical, psychological — but I did it, and my older sister was able to get away and road trip with me. Otherwise, I don't know that I would have been able to do it. I just couldn't imagine myself there alone, and welp, if I can't imagine it, it just doesn't happen.

The last time I visited Maine was when my dad got remarried, in 2002. And before that … it was the summer before I turned 16, so 1982? Sheesh. When I decide to have complicated relationships with places, I go all in.

In '02, Mark came with me. We'd landed in Boston and moseyed up from there. I had a little breakdown in a motel, I remember. Just couldn't stop crying. Lying in bed, tears in my ears, totally silent, perfectly normal. Mark was already exhibiting symptoms of the cancer he wouldn't see a doctor about until September of '04, and which killed him four years after that.

Ah, memories.

In '82, I was in the midst of a serious depressive episode and dealing with yet another diet from my doctor, which was starving me. Our parents had left us there that year, with old friends of theirs, for two weeks, so they could maybe (I'm pretty sure) salvage their marriage. It didn't go great for me, I guess.

But that's perhaps a story for another day, if I ever figure it out. Because Maine is magical. It smells amazing, it's beautiful. Their new state slogan is on stickers and patches at every souvenir shop: The Way Life Should Be. It's hard to argue that. In each "crowd" of people -- at the farmer's market, in the lovely tourist town, by the water -- I was hard pressed to find a single person looking at their phone. I'm from Los Angeles. Let's just say I wasn't in Kansas anymore.

Maine forces you to slow down. Nothing can be done in a hurry. You can get there from here, but you should be sure to leave plenty of time.

Of course, we only had a few days. And who knows how long Dad has? I don't know what to hope for, so I guess it's good that hoping doesn't get you much. He's not going to get better. I don't want to do without him, but he's living my idea of hell. I felt the same way about Mark in the end. If I have to do without you so you can be free of this, I'm willing. Not that any of it is up to me.

And it makes you think things like, *What the fuck am I doing?* and *Is this all there is?* And I know you're not supposed to make big decisions when you're grieving, but I'm 53, I'm always grieving something, and that little maxim is also a good excuse to ignore things that are trying to push you forward. My life has gotten so very, very small. I can't seem to make it bigger. Historically, I moved to new cities when I felt like this, and I can't help thinking it's long past time for me to do that again. To shake up the snow globe a little bit. I don't think anyone would truthfully say I've wrung every bit out of LA, but I think I need to come to terms with the fact that I'm not going to.

The thing is, I take after my dad, much more so than my sisters. We don't really move on our own, he and I, we need other people to move us. And he married people with forceful personalities, I think because he knew on some level it would be the only way he'd get anywhere. Not that he got anywhere. Old age comes for us all, if we're "lucky," but he was never what you'd call successful -— in business or in marriage. He's a deeply good guy, but historically all too content to let life happen around him, and he never had the wherewithal to effect any real change on his own. And the change that was visited upon him by those forceful personalities wasn't his. It was theirs, and that was fine with him, because he didn't have any other strong feelings.

I'm full of strong feelings, but no ability to do anything about them. And part of my wishful wondering about a partner is about someone to help pull me forward, no matter what direction. Someone just tell me what to do.

Not Run Down Enough

LAST WEEK, I CAME home to a note on my door from a location scout. This is the second time this has happened. The first time, the man — who without a second thought I let into the house I live alone in to take copious photos — just loved my kitchen, and lamented how hard it is to find unrenovated kitchens like mine. Well, look no further! There's nary a stainless steel appliance to be found! And let's not forget the knotty pine cabinets my landlord built and installed all by himself, shoddily. Take in the layers upon layers of linoleum on the floor. You can really see the history of the place in these ragged edges, because he never pulled up the old stuff before putting the new flooring down, and he never installed any trim. Here's the fake brick, the tiny stovetop just a hair too small for the hole he cut in the tile, and the broken dial on the oven. It's *perfect*.

Anyhoo, they were interested in my house for the scene in which the hero finds the dead body.

It was just as well they never called. I might have been able to withstand the shame, but I'd have had to deal with my landlord, and only the prospect of decent money could have done that. But he'd likely have taken most or all the money, so I was glad nothing came of it.

So I didn't have high hopes last week when I saw the little note from the scout wondering if I'd be interested. I texted him the next night.

"Hi, you left a note at my house yesterday. Haha, it looks pretty run down, if that helps jog your memory."

His answer? "Unfortunately, it's not run down enough."

Imagine my elation. Too good for the meth lab flashback scene? This is amazing!

But he was still typing. "We need the whole neighborhood to look that way. Yours is a bit too nice for this movie."

To be clear, my house is indeed just right, it's just my neighbors that are ruining my big break. I'll make sure to tell them so.

I've made a big Life Decision; I'm seriously planning to leave Los Angeles. It feels big to me, but no one I tell is reacting with very much surprise. It's clear that I absolutely need to go, but aren't they the slightest bit impressed that I'm actually doing it? Maybe they don't think I will. Can't blame them there. I've had a lot of big ideas, and they know better than anyone that I'm not brave. I'm terrified of both dying by violence and wearing sleeveless shirts. The prospect of getting naked in front of someone is as awful to me as the prospect of living the rest of my life alone — no lie, that seesaw is completely level.

Despite all this, I've finally begun to see change on the horizon, and maybe because of this, work is harder. Something has shifted; I'm on an edge. There's nothing about it I want to do, my only concern is how badly I'm faking it. I think a lot about giving my notice. And because the things I've wanted this badly historically have not happened, I can only dread the fall when the (really vague) job opportunity never comes to fruition. It's a weird, familiar, sad perch.

As much as it stings, and no matter what happens with this job prospect, I need to leave LA. In part, I need to escape the witnesses to my ridiculous half-life. (*Don't look at me*, the thing in the hovel hisses. *I'm hideous.*) If this opportunity doesn't work out, then I'll find a different, more affordable city and go there.

My small little life is a lot like this house, I suppose, suffering by comparison to everything that surrounds it. Honestly, the only question is why it took so long to make this decision. I guess I just wasn't run down enough.

Bit Part: Fired Up

THE WILDFIRES IN CALIFORNIA are a seasonal mindfuck. I find them deeply unsettling, but that should come as no surprise. I don't do well with things that are raging out of control. Sometimes they are abstract, far away. Sometimes the car is covered in ash. We're breathing in people's homes, their livelihoods.

The news organizations fill a lot of space with fire news, and I remember vividly a photo of a man with a garden hose, his body silhouetted against the fire on the mountain behind his home, a wall of angry orange. I think about him all the time.

Why was he still there with his tiny hose, a feeble trickle of water his only defense against what would surely be the inevitable fate of his home? What was he *doing?*

But what else *could* he do? Turn off the water? Is the answer really to throw down your only weapon? While I am basically wired to give in, even I know this: because the fire rages is no reason to turn off the hose.

Things Left Behind

ONE OF THE EDITORS of this book suggested that it might a good idea to discuss some things I gave up, in hopes of illustrating how meaningful it can be to let go of things that aren't worth your energy or effort. But compiling a list of everything I've given up on was unexpectedly painful and revelatory. Because the answer is everything.

If we start with early, school-age stuff, then I can tell you I excelled at almost nothing in an academic space. Not one science; no languages; not music, be it theory, song, or playing an instrument (six full years of violin, and, in desperation, a year of flute); not math beyond basic algebra, which I had to take a second time because I was in danger of failing geometry. In college, I failed a biology class my first semester, and I struggled to recover from that for the rest of my time there. I poked around for another course of study and made halfhearted stabs at humanities and art. I was completely overwhelmed by philosophy, since I couldn't tell one of those wordy men from another and classes were mostly debates I felt unequal to and frustrated by. As an adult, I continued the search for something I could do well, and I tried photography (multiple times); violin (again, those poor violins);

languages (recall that I grew up listening to Spanish conversation). I gave up on all of it.

I took honors English classes in high school but never the AP courses. I could inexplicably understand Shakespeare, but most poetry was impenetrable. It seems clear that thanks to rehearsals and repetition, my work on stage could be more fully understood than anything else I attempted, and it had the extra benefit of audience laughter and applause. I felt good at it, which is probably all it boils down to in the end. I was desperate for that.

I have complained in these pages about my seeming unwillingness to proceed down a path when the goal is too big. I am facing the hard truth that most goals are too big for me. When met with a complex system of any type, there is only so far I can go. I used to think it was laziness, but when I really think about what happens in my brain — the wall I slam into when attempting to embrace anything remotely complicated — then I have to allow that there may be a learning disability in the mix.

It is a comfort to think that it's not laziness or self-sabotage, nor is it a failing of will. It reframes my view, explains why I turned away from those workplace advancements or offered opportunities, how willing I have always been to take the path of least resistance. It explains my sense of always being on the outside.

It boggles my mind when I listen to a learned person talk about their subject of expertise. How did they *do* that?

There are other things in the mix here, none of them particularly painless. As I've done the unpacking work on myself and my experiences, it's hard not to notice that a list of my personality traits corresponds uncomfortably with a list of childhood trauma symptoms. Hi there, hypervigilance, anxiety, sleeplessness, intrusive thoughts, self-criticism, distorted beliefs, social withdrawal, trouble making decisions, prioritizing the needs of others, and *oversharing of personal details*. Thanks for the book.

There is a short list of things I'm good at. I'm a decent knitter, though I'm overwhelmed by larger projects. I enjoy puzzles of various kinds. I can read something and answer questions about it afterwards, which is what got me through school as an ostensible success. But I don't hold onto most of that knowledge. Other than putting words together (in the English language only), there's no true skill or passion I can hang my hat on, no nuanced understanding of any complicated topic.

Most of these written pieces aren't true essays, and when that was pointed out, I revised the subtitle of this book rather than fix that. I can feel my way, grammatically speaking, but don't ask me to explain what a participle is. Don't make me look up *predicate* again.

I can't retain information about historical events, positions on a map, legal principles. Don't give me directions that include cardinal points. I look the same things up again and again. For example, I just had to look up *cardinal*. It's a running joke at work that I still don't quite understand how we do what we do, and I've been there for almost five years. My defense is that I don't need to know. I do the widget work of scheduling meetings, arranging for travel, and submitting purchasing forms. I am good at it, and I know it's valuable, but I am aware that my work is made up of very small, very simple tasks.

I can see now that as someone who didn't often understand what was being said, I instead focused on the how and why things were being said, and by whom. I get (to a degree) how humans deal with each other, their feelings and failings. And since I couldn't understand, I focused on being understood. These are all puzzles. Writing is puzzle solving.

It's taken me *years* to put this book together. I put it away for months at a stretch because, frankly, it got too big and unwieldy for me to manage. The editor notes killed my will to move forward. So, so much to do, to work through, to make sense of, never mind that you must constantly relive and re-examine all your failures and saddest stories. I had to break this manuscript down into the smallest possible chunks, something that most writers advise — in this, at least, I know I'm not alone — but I would have been happy to put it away forever had I not told so many people I would do it. It would have been such a relief. I cannot imagine ever putting pen to paper again, which echoes back across the years. Writing may well be added to a very long list.

So much mortification this rush of insight brings with it, but it is, at least, clarifying. It explains why new bodies of knowledge only frustrate, why it was so hard to find my creative place, why I hand my power over to almost anyone else so they can be in charge.

It casts new light on almost everything I've written about so far, but it will also inform the future, which is a good thing. It's good information to have.

While it does help to think that maybe all my failures aren't about character, necessarily, it is enormously painful to think about all the frustration and wasted time. I feel like I'm in mourning, in a sense. I used to joke that the childhood photos of me always look like something terrible happened in the moments just before. Now, my heart breaks for that little girl. She's just lost.

Consolation

THE BUTTERFLIES PASSED THROUGH. They were beautiful, little fluttery things migrating from Mexico by the many thousands. My office is on the fourth floor, and I noted them passing but didn't get curious about it for a few days. Every one of them were heading north, not a single rebel in the bunch. They hit their peak one day — I could count a hundred or more in under a minute — and then the next day, abruptly, they were done.

It was so ... sweet. Sort of adorable and innocent, just doing what they do. Their numbers were cause for celebration, a bumper crop after recent sharp decreases in populations, but the bad news is built in. An unexpected leap forward into a deeply uncertain future. Uncertain is probably too tame a word, too hopeful for what is really happening.

There's been a lot of bad news lately, just a relentless deluge of crappy things. I didn't plan on seeing the end of the Earth, or even the end of the republic, for that matter. I'm not sure what I'm meant to be doing while all this is going on. What tune should we be fiddling while Rome burns? Everything I do feels like wasted time.

Still, it seems wise to disconnect from the noise of it all, if that's even possible, but as much as I really can tell the difference on days

when I'm not fixated on my social media feeds, it feels cowardly. I
don't know how to balance knowing what's happening with not
knowing what to do about it. And everywhere, everywhere, there
are people acting as if everything is normal. Planning trips, making
babies, it's mind boggling.

"Don't worry," people say, "Things have always been terrible.
The doomsayers have always predicted doom." But the Earth is
dying. There's a massive species die-off. Look at the flooding,
the storms. What was awful before was fixable, we even made
progress, albeit at a snail's pace. The people who could fix this now
absolutely refuse to. Our democracy is on the brink — minority
rule is in our immediate future, it's already happening. And to
shrug right now and say it will all work out is to say it will all
work out for *you*. People are dying who don't have to, entire groups
are intentionally oppressed, and our leaders have always had the
power to stop it and never have. We don't deserve nice things; look
what we've done with our gifts.

My sister came for a nice long visit, and it did occur to me that
disconnecting from certain things allows for connecting to others.
I called it the Consolation Tour — Elena and I took advantage of
many of them: art, music, comedy, nature. It was a lovely time and
a good reminder. And at each venue, each open space, I was struck
by all the other people present, who had gathered to see or hear
beautiful things. These are congregations, my kind of congregants.
I believe all these things could restore us on a larger scale, but for
now they can only help some of us feel better for a little while.

There's a lesson in everything. The butterflies rebounded. Why,
oh why, can't I? What if I committed to doing the things I do

best, stopped lamenting and started fucking writing? Okay, so I can't save the world, but I probably wasn't meant to. Being part of what consoles others would probably (maybe, might) console me. Maybe I can only fly north. I don't have to know why or where the path will lead. But I should goddamn do it.

Being Green

WHEN MY MOTHER WAS ill, in the late 1980s, she watched a lot of Sesame Street. We had what was probably first-generation cable. If memory serves, the channels were letters ... can that be right? Anyway, she had choices, but she'd always been an avid supporter of public television, and she chose Sesame Street.

We were a Children's Television Network kind of family. We partook of all the offerings: Mister Roger's Neighborhood, Electric Company, you name it. Bob McGrath, an actor on Sesame Street, lived in my hometown of Teaneck, New Jersey, and my younger sister was the same age as his daughter. She played at their house! One day I called there to see if my sister had left for home yet, and I got completely tongue-tied when I realized I was talking to Bob. *The* Bob. From Sesame Street, answering his own phone.

I have such fond memories of that show. It was a constant in my, at times, confusing childhood. And while it's true that the TV was often my babysitter, Sesame Street has a special place for me. I still have warm feelings for the people who kept me company. It's an impressive list, including Ray Charles, The Count, Gordon, Lena Horne, Prairie Dawn, Lily Tomlin, Big Bird, and Guy Smiley (the best Muppet name ever).

It's not that easy being green
Having to spend each day the color of the leaves
When I think it could be nicer being red, or yellow or gold
Or something much more colorful like that

On my mother's gravestone, under her name, it says "Artist, Wife, Mother." She was first and foremost an artist, and a brilliant one, but a difficult personality and hard to live with. When her symptoms first appeared, she adjusted. She moved from printmaking to watercolors and collage. But eventually she couldn't do those things either. She was diagnosed with multiple sclerosis, but I should tell you there were no half measures with that woman; she never had a mild case of anything. True to form, she got hit hard. She couldn't walk much of the time. She had blurry vision, her hands were numb and shaky, and her memory got increasingly bad. She would usually get our names right, but she'd also obsess over certain things and return to them repeatedly. "That stupid man, my father," she'd say, over and over. For a long time, she'd keep telling you the color of her eyes, which were a beautiful hazel green. And she'd repeat everything she heard, even the announcements over the paging system when she was at the hospital. "Dr. Patel, extension 2541," she'd say, in the exact same inflection as the voice of the pager. When a patient down the hall would yell for the nurse, Mom's voice would follow immediately after. "Nurse!"

She also benefited from the Spanish language instruction on Sesame Street, and she would practice it all the time.

"Mom, are you ready for lunch?"

"Sí."

Or, "How many cookies would you like?"

"Dos."

Once she said, about something or other, "Wunderbar." Then a pause. "I don't know why I'm speaking Spanish all of a sudden."

We were like, "Ma, that was German."

"It *was?*"

My dad moved his business home, into what had been her basement studio. If she needed something, she'd call his office number from the bedroom phone upstairs. Once, he came home from an errand and found this collection of messages, all left within a few minutes of each other:

Beep. "Pete? It's a little cold up here, would you bring me a blanket?"

Beep. "It's me. Pretty chilly, when you get a chance."

Beep. "Pete, are you there? Still need that blanket, I'm cold."

Beep. "It's not easy being green."

I told you she was really into that show. But this phrase came up again and again. She said it all the time. And it seems significant to me. It's one of my favorite songs ever. Just the simplest, most beautiful argument for being who you are that I know of. It was written by Joe Raposo, and though first made famous by Kermit the Frog, it's been covered by Frank Sinatra, Tony Bennett, Ray Charles, Diana Ross, Bob McGrath and Oscar the Grouch, to name just a few, but the standout version for me is by Van Morrison.

Joe Raposo died young, just like my mother did, and in the same year, 1989. Studies done that year about the song, which made its debut in the first season of Sesame Street, indicated that most little kids didn't get the fact that Kermit ends up happy about his greenness. They come away with the idea that it's all melancholy. And thinking back, I might have felt like that too. I know I didn't love it then like I love it now. And it's probably because of Van Morrison that I ever realized what an amazing song it is. His version will give you the chills.

It's not easy being green
It seems you blend in with so many other ordinary things
And people tend to pass you by 'cause you're
Not standing out like flashy sparkles in the water
Or stars in the sky

My mother was not a gentle teacher, but her lessons were good ones. And maybe because she died at the age of 47 — way before I had even begun to make peace with her — I read too much into the little things at the end. Even so. She knew how to be who she was. It wasn't all that easy for us kids to be who we were, what with her being who she was all over the place. But she was better at accepting herself than most people I know. Certainly better than I've been at accepting me. But this song teaches you, over and over, since it's somehow so easy to forget, that there's another side to the being you coin that is completely and unequivocally awesome, no matter who you are. And she said the title a hundred times before she died. It seems to me that even if that doesn't mean anything, it's okay to pretend it does.

Because green's the color of Spring,

and green can be cool and friendly-like.
It can be big like an ocean,
or important like a mountain,
or tall like a tree

There was a special done for Jim Henson a little while after he died. In it, Fozzie Bear gets a note from Kermit asking that the Muppets put together a tribute to Henson. But none of them know who he is. (Cue heartbreak.) So they talk to friends of his like Steven Spielberg, John Denver, and Frank Oz. And there are home movies and early show clips from the Muppets before there was Sesame Street. In the end, they plan a big production number with Vikings, a whoopee cushion, and some marching accountants. But then they find a stack of condolence letters from little kids to Kermit, with their little drawings and everything, saying how sorry they are that his friend died. But this was a blow — they hadn't realized he was dead. And Gonzo says, "But we were just getting to know him!" And now that he sees how beloved Henson was, Fozzie loses faith in the production number being a fitting memorial. But wee Robin the Frog convinces him, and they all join in on a song called "Just One Person." Big Bird shows up, and finally Kermit himself. I cried and cried.

We should pay tribute to the people who helped form us, so I'm here to thank Jim Henson, Joe Raposo, and Florence Noa. Who all caught on early, thank goodness, about who they were and what they would spend their lives doing. I'm years past the age my mother was when she died, and I've barely even gotten started. And it sometimes feels like I've wasted a lot of valuable time worrying about things I can't do anything about. But I guess I shouldn't worry about that either.

When green is all there is to be,
it could make you wonder why,
but why? Why wonder why?
I am green and it'll do fine.
And it's what I want to be.

(**'Bein' Green,'** by Joe Raposo, used by permission of The Joe Raposo Music Group, Inc.)

TL; DR

Written for the last show I did in LA
before moving, at the Fanatic Salon.

APOLOGIES IN ADVANCE, BUT I will probably cry. I don't think anyone comes out to comedy shows to cry, necessarily, or watch someone else do it, but hey, we're here now so let's just see how it goes. (Also, the door is locked.) But I'm emotional. After more than 20 years, I am leaving Los Angeles.

When I first started doing essays, they were funnier. Used to be they were just funny, then they were mostly humorous with a little something to think about. Now, they're a candy-coated chemo pill. So, again, apologies. But I've grown older, life has happened, as much as I tried to hide. I'm maybe wiser, definitely scarred, and I want everything to be meaningful, and sometimes that's not haha funny.

I don't believe in a single thing *out there*. About where we're going or what happens after this. I only have faith in the idea that we humans — each of us beating astronomical odds to even be here — are all connected. And the evidence for me has been found in little theaters like this, where a particular congregation gathers for the first and only time to witness something that will never happen again. They call it ephemeral art, but it can have a lasting effect. I need to believe that, because I'm leaving, and I'm afraid it'll be like I was never here.

We moved here in 1999, my late husband and I, full of unrealistic dreams. Six winters in Chicago had slowed our metabolisms and forward motion, and his job transfer seemed like a gift. I had an MFA in Acting. Not a particularly good one, but still. I wasn't auditioning in Chicago, and I didn't know why, but I thought maybe the answer might be found somewhere else. And it was, just not the one I wanted.

I'm hard wired to think very little of myself. This is the kindest way I can put it, and I'm not fishing for compliments. They don't work. This disorder is under the OCD umbrella, so my internal messaging is particularly relentless. It only shuts up when I am on stage, as it happens, but afterward it comes rushing back with a vengeance and makes me regret everything I said, what I wore, how I looked. I won't be able to fall asleep tonight with all that in my head. I can't make you understand, but I can tell you it's gotten worse over time. It's practically cellular, and it affects every part of my life. And you can tell. You may not know exactly what's wrong, but anyone armed with even two facts about my life can tell that something is off.

By the way, if you're over forty and still telling yourself that you have foibles or weird habits or idiosyncrasies, it's more likely what you have are conditions and syndromes and disorders. It's a painful realization, but sometimes a relief, and the sooner you figure this stuff out, the clearer you can be about the paths that are realistically open to you. I came to LA doomed. I pre-failed at this, but I was thirty-two. I still thought success would be about effort and opportunities. I wondered a lot about what was wrong with me, but I wasn't diagnosed till ten or so years ago, and the nature of this particular disorder makes it almost impossible to be compassionate with myself. It also makes it difficult to audition, to date anyone, or to find a new job. You can't sell a product you don't believe in.

I never had a chance in LA. What I wanted was to be seen and heard, but that's a tough ask when you also don't want anyone to look at you. We all want validation, but I require it since I can't trust what's going on in my head. But what's going on in my head makes it impossible for me to even get headshots taken or submit them to agents.

It's good, even necessary, to shake things loose, clean the slate. I grew up in New Jersey, then I lived in Pennsylvania for college and grad school, then I went to Chicago, where there were so many more professional theaters, then to Los Angeles, where ... hm. Where what, exactly? I don't know. I did not have a plan. It's hard to look back at who I was then, even though I'm prone and even pathologically wired to look back. I'm made of nostalgia, and past a certain age, that rear view is unavoidably painful. I came here hoping, like everyone else. And I leave here relieved, because I can finally, finally stop hoping.

It's been twenty flipping years. I've overstayed, and I'm amazed it didn't occur to me till now. The person I came here with is long dead. That car, those pets, the dream, gone. I'm living in the rental house we shared, surrounded by the stuff we settled on, hand-me-downs and bargain basement finds.

I've always had problems leaving places. After shows, I end up locking up the theater at the end of the night. At parties, I'll be doing your dishes after everyone else leaves. And always there's my usual social remorse over that. *Why did I stay so long? What is wrong with me?* But on the rare occasion I do leave early, it's: *Did I remember to say a proper goodbye to everyone? Was I awkward or rude?*

When it comes to leaving a workplace, I must be either forced out or moving to a different state. It's best when I can blame the leaving on the move. Because I don't want to ever tell someone who cares about me that I am leaving anyway. I am reminded (literally all the time) of Dorothy on the yellow brick road. It's different when you have to go. No offense, Scarecrow, but home isn't here.

Historically, moving away for me equals moving forward. It's important for me to get away from the weight of other people's expectations, which makes it very hard for me to feel like I can effect any meaningful, visible change. I can't stand the fishbowl; I don't want to grow where everyone can see me, which I know is part of my disorder. It's why I like reading essays at shows like this. I arrive fully formed, no stumbling steps. Like a crow. You never see baby crows, they just appear, ready for anything. Scrappy, fierce, *confident.*

It felt huge to me when I finally decided to leave, but it seemed like everyone I told was waiting for exactly this. Their reactions were so encouraging and calm, almost … careful. Like, "Don't spook her, just nod. She needs to go." The voice in my head suggests that they've been discussing it among themselves. *Why is she still here?*

I don't know! But almost every sign seems to be pointing the way out of town.

The job search was a terribly painful process, a dredging up of such ugly internal sludge even I was surprised, and I'm well-versed in my internal sludge. As in casting, you must convince a total stranger that you're perfect for a role you don't know anything about, and I've never once felt the best at anything. Presenting myself for approval is the thing I'm worst at. *Clinically.* That's been the problem this whole time. Now, I know I'm a good employee, but I also know that that's largely because I'm afraid not to be. I've kept myself low partly because I clung to the idea that these were just day jobs, but partly, I suspect, so that I can more easily exceed expectations.

I should be clear, the only reason I got this new gig is because a friend was advocating for me from the inside. I couldn't get my foot in the door any other way. And I want it, of course I do. It's much better money, and it gets me out of town. I can do the work. It's just hard to feel like I deserve it. I've been patient and well-behaved, sure, and I've long complained about the fact that there's no reward for good behavior other than a shining record of good behavior. But this feels like a prize for sitting very still. For being a coward.

It was hard to even say I wanted the job. I've been living so long in a state of reactive readiness. I can't remember the last time I effected the next big change in my life. That's the triumph here. I'd been hiding for years. To say I wanted something felt like putting myself in the worst sort of danger. I felt exposed, vulnerable to attack. How dare you, Jenny? How dare *you*, of all people?

The new company is in a good place, but it's a startup, which is certainly riskier than I'm used to. The recruitment process has been somewhat grueling, and it might have come with one or two red flags. It's not perfect, but nothing is, and no one settles like I do. It's on my list of special skills.

We talked a lot about my move during the interview process, and I had an epiphany literally while talking to my new boss. I'm still living in the story of my husband's illness and death, my subsequent layoff and unemployment, and the slow climb out of that hole. I'm still in it, still wading through the dust of our naïve plans while I watch my friends continue on in pursuit of something I still yearn for. You might say LA has kicked my ass. It's not a happy story. Screw a new chapter, I need to close that book, set it on fire, and start a new one. It really is out of my hands.

So, farewell. Thank you. It hurts to pull up roots that are 20 years deep. But that doesn't mean you shouldn't do it, especially when a thing is growing in the wrong place. Despite the shitty things that happened here, I love Los Angeles, and I always will. I'm more grateful than I can say to you and the others like you, who came out to see shows like this on faith. I hope I've held up my end of the bargain. It's meant everything to me.

I'm finally right for the role, one of a middle-aged woman who lucks into a well-paying position after a long career of low-level office day jobs and a flimsy hope of discovery in a town that was never looking for her in the first place. Who, against all odds and just past her prime, gets her very first taste of financial security. Along the way, she'll have to overcome crushing guilt about who gets to win in this world while so many lose, and she'll be screamed at the whole time by the voices in her head who actively hate her and sabotage her happiness. But hey, she'll be able to travel more, and she won't have full-blown anxiety attacks over the cost of routine vet visits for her cat — and her little dog, too. By the end of the story, she'll come to realize that people do plays and make art and music and write whole books in places that are not Los Angeles, and she'll learn what happens when the pressure is off and it's just about what she creates and not whether it will support her and how she looks and who she's wearing. Oh, and the ideal candidate for this role will have BROWN CURLY HAIR and BROWN EYES and weigh whatever the fuck she wants.

The Other Side

I won't sugarcoat this: moving was among the harder things I've ever done. I know that it's one of the major life stresses, but the fact that strangers had to come and see my mess and pack up the art and transfer my zillion boxes to a new location all took more of a toll than I was prepared for. But I did it. It beat the crap out of me, but I faced the demon.

My apartment is beige, the very beigest in all the land. But I'm comfortable. I feel safe in my own space, far safer than I ever managed in that house in LA. I feel less exposed, less accessible.

The job is good. It still doesn't feel real. We went into lockdown five weeks after I started, so there was some anxiety there, to be sure. I just put my head down, and I made sure to volunteer for anything I thought I could help with. I was deeply insecure for the best part of the year, thanks to telecommuting and because my boss is somewhat taciturn, but mostly because I'm me. My issues are still very much here.

But I finally started to relax into it and can trust that it's going well. It's the first job I ever took where I wasn't already thinking about when I might be able to leave, and that's incredibly refreshing. I didn't even know that was a thing. It's not my day job; it's my job.

They pay me well, and it's impossible to overstate what an important piece of the puzzle that is for me. I am still constantly aware of how lucky I feel on that score, and how much of a change it is. The enormous financial worry weight has been lifted. It's no small thing. I'm not one of those writers. There's no romance for me in the writing-in-a-garret-with-just-a-crust-of-bread-for-dinner scenario. I need stability.

I think a lot about what might be created if more people felt secure enough to do it.

There was a desperation to my previous creative efforts, a hope that they might save me. If only I did this, I could stop doing that. That's a hard way to start. I was never going to produce anything worthwhile from where I was. How can you report on a hole from inside it?

I work with people who are not only among the best in the world at what they do, but are *doing it*. Impossible not to set that next to LA, where so many people you meet, who are also enormously talented and extremely hard working, aren't able to do the work they want to and wish that things were different.

I am projecting, mostly. But I wrote this book, and it couldn't have happened before. (We know because it didn't.) I am inspired by my new coworkers to, like them, own what I am good at and put effort in. There is no benefit to anyone if I don't create in the way that makes sense to me. I'm doing this on my terms. It's clear to me now that I was also insisting on "my terms" in LA; it's just that in LA, my terms looked a lot like losing. There's no need now for anyone else to validate what I do or give me permission to proceed.

There are a lot of good and honest and talented creators in LA who, for their own reasons, are also driven to win against all odds. That's a lot. But you can create elsewhere. Not for those big paychecks, not for that huge audience. But very few people get either of those things.

I am happier now than I can remember being, and all I had to do was give up my dreams. This has the advantage of being true, sad, and funny — my favorite combination. My choice was to be sad about everything, or happy about everything except that one thing. The pain is more about not realizing this sooner than about any real grief about the loss itself. You can't grieve what was never possible. It's just a story I told myself, one I've grown out of and away from.

People love to hate it, but Los Angeles is a beautifully creative place, and not just in ways connected to the movie industry. Whatever your interest, you can find or form a group of like-minded artists or craftspeople. That is objectively good to my mind, but it was hard too, to watch all those people go after their Things, while I slogged away in office jobs I had no real connection to but somehow couldn't sacrifice.

There are, not surprisingly, no guides for getting out, for letting go. But the idea that you might need to is hard to accept among those still engaged in the quest. Peculiarly, a stated intention to stop trying is met with a lot of resistance. Everyone has their own reasons for sticking with it or letting it go, but there's a perceived sense of abandonment. (We were all in this fun, creative boat! It's inherently cool!) But it's complicated.

A painter can paint regardless of gallery interest. A dancer benefits in myriad ways from dancing whether or not it's a career. But an actor needs an audience — to make a living but also to get better at it. And anyone who dreamed of audiences larger than a handful of people at their improv show (in essence, every actor) will be, to varying degrees, disappointed in their reach and impact. Or maybe they get lucky in that they just don't think about it. They don't obsess over it. They just press on. Which is truly admirable. It's just not, alas, me.

I want to say that success in LA is a roll of the dice, but it's more of a slot machine. You feed in your money and your time and your youth, and you hope for a jackpot. Because you must. And while it's true that the dream can happen for anyone, it's also true that it can't happen for everyone.

I am hard on myself, but spelling it all out like this, I accept that I wasn't doing nothing for two decades. Inarguably, some things got in the way. But I also never fought for the things I wanted in the way I think they deserved. In the way you'd need to if you ever want to get anything seen or made.

I don't know that I chose to leap as much as I was pushed, but I won't quibble. I am content. I feel equal to the tasks before me. When you're generally unhappy, almost everything feels like a burden. But when you're generally happy, almost nothing does. Another of my many revelations.

There are bad days, naturally. Knowing your brain isn't working as it should is not great, and disordered thinking has tentacles that burrow deep. But even if that knowledge doesn't magically stop the spiral, knowing what's happening can help you find patience to get to the end. It is not a secret weapon, but a vital piece of information when on the battlefield.

With distance and time, I can see just how depressed I was in the last years. I mean, I knew I was, that's part of my disorder cocktail. But a lot of the frustration I was feeling and the behavior I was reporting had more to do with that than I realized. When you're low for long enough, it just feels normal. I didn't know the problem was solvable. I thought I would always have to fight the same-sized monster, and I'm finding that the monster is much, much smaller and less scary. Maybe I just have a better arsenal.

The LA experience was ultimately a long process of letting go of that original dream. That one that was never going to happen anyway. I'm amazed how long it took, but excising something so much a part of you is a big job. Hope is so stubborn, and grief isn't a linear process. This was not a straight shot from *I shouldn't be doing this* to *I've stopped doing this*. It was a painful, circuitous route. I did not want to let go of those things.

As I considered leaving LA, I felt like a little kid threatening to run away. "That's it, I'm leaving. This is me going now. Here I go ... iiiinnnn five, four ...." It's hard for me to leave places. It's hard for me to let go of complicated relationships, and LA is nothing if not complicated. It was part of a pattern, I see now. I was stalling in hopes that someone or something would give me a reason to stay. No matter how much dousing a fire gets, there's a little ember that stays warm. The first spark never goes out.

This might be why I failed for so long to fill in the space those dreams had occupied, which led to some missteps and backtracking. There's probably no good way to do this. Given the chance to try again, I'm not sure I could do it any differently.

I've always been stymied by the journey. I want to be there, but I don't want to get there. I want to see the view from the summit, but I have no interest in, or perhaps too much fear of, the climb. And in those anxieties lurk all the real issues — what I deserve as a human being on this Earth. And what this body, in particular, deserves. It's a slog. But it's a slog I'm undertaking far away from that enraging, inspiring, depressing, seductive town.

Who You (Happen to) Know

I HAVE SAID THIS for ages. It's not who you get to know — the ones you schmooze at parties or networking events. It's the people you came up with, took classes with, did shows with. They are your People. And I got very lucky. My time in Los Angeles, for all its personal frustrations and challenges, was nevertheless peopled by a cast of interesting and funny characters I was lucky to know and honored to play with.

I am particularly indebted to the creative community I found at bang. improv studio, late of the Fairfax district, founded by Aliza and Peter Murrieta. I've said it before — every good thing that happened to me in LA, creatively speaking, grew from bang. Thank you for the many good times in class and out, on stage and off. Thanks to Gaye Coffman for dragging this extremely reluctant future improvisor to that first class. I'm more grateful than I can say.

Thank you to the incredible live storytelling community in Los Angeles. And I owe a particular debt of gratitude to Christine Schoenwald, whose producing, mentorship and encouragement opened the door to this kind of work for me and so many others.

A giant hug to the regular audience members and fans: to everyone who came to the shows, to the strangers who stayed after to chat, and to my friends who showed up time and again.

Grateful thanks to The Big Hollywood Big Time Big Shots, some of my favorite people ever. We should do a sketch show!

Special thanks to Karen C., for listening so well to all the things I wrote, and for so patiently seeing me through the process of letting go of Los Angeles.

Warm thanks to my editors as well as the beta, sensitivity, and ARC readers. Handing over the work is so hard. Thank you for taking such good care of it.

To my sisters, Lisa and Elena, all my love.

About the Author

Jenny Noa lives and works in the Bay Area. You may find more information, join her mailing list, or reach out directly at www.jennynoa.com.

Made in the USA
Las Vegas, NV
23 November 2024

12485351R00154